Our Edible Toadstools and Mushrooms

And How To Distinguish Them

by

William Hamilton Gibson

APPLEWOOD BOOKS
Bedford, Massachusetts

Our Edible Toadstools and Mushrooms

was originally published in

1895

ISBN: 978-1-4290-1263-8

Thank you for purchasing an Applewood book.
Applewood reprints America's lively classics—
books from the past that are still of interest
to the modern reader.
For a free copy of
a catalog of our
bestselling
books,
write
to us at:
Applewood Books
Box 365
Bedford, MA 01730
or visit us on the web at:
For cookbooks: foodsville.com
For our complete catalog: awb.com

Prepared for publishing by HP

Our Edible Mushrooms

The Deadly "Amanita".

Our Edible Toadstools and Mushrooms
and
How to Distinguish Them

A Selection of Thirty Native Food Varieties Easily Recognizable by their Marked Individualities, with Simple Rules for the Identification of Poisonous Species

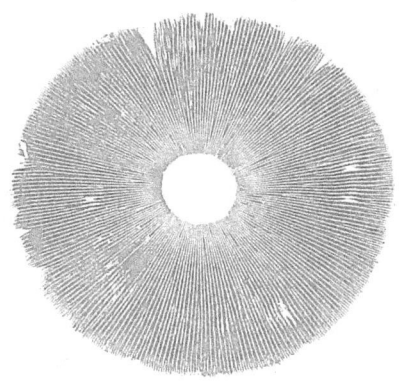

By W. HAMILTON GIBSON

WITH THIRTY COLORED PLATES
AND FIFTY-SEVEN OTHER ILLUSTRATIONS BY THE AUTHOR

NEW YORK
HARPER & BROTHERS PUBLISHERS
1895

THE WORKS OF W. HAMILTON GIBSON.

ILLUSTRATED BY THE AUTHOR.

SHARP EYES. A Rambler's Calendar among Birds, Insects, and Flowers. 8vo, $5 00.
HIGHWAYS AND BYWAYS; or, Saunterings in New England. 4to, $7 50.
STROLLS BY STARLIGHT AND SUNSHINE. Royal 8vo, $3 50.
HAPPY HUNTING-GROUNDS. A Tribute to the Woods and Fields. 4to, $7 50.
PASTORAL DAYS; or, Memories of a New England Year. 4to, $7 50.
CAMP LIFE IN THE WOODS, and the Tricks of Trapping and Trap-making. 16mo, $1 00.

PUBLISHED BY HARPER & BROTHERS, NEW YORK.

Copyright, 1895, by HARPER & BROTHERS.

All rights reserved.

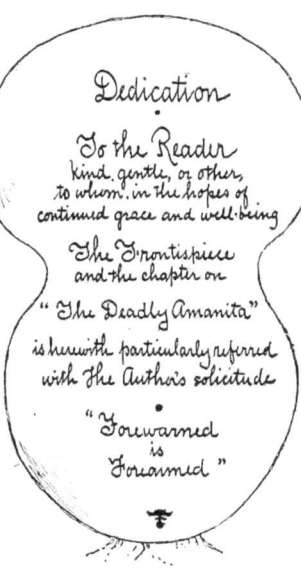

Dedication

To the Reader
kind, gentle, or other,
to whom, in the hopes of
continued grace and well-being

The Frontispiece
and the chapter on

"The Deadly Amanita"

is herewith particularly referred
with The Author's solicitude

"Forewarned
is
Forearmed"

For those who do hunger after the earthlie excrescences called mushrooms.''—GERARDE.

Contents

	Page
INTRODUCTION	1
THE DEADLY AMANITA	43
THE AGARICACEÆ	77
THE POLYPOREI	181
MISCELLANEOUS FUNGI	231
SPORE-PRINTS	277
RECIPES	299
BIBLIOGRAPHY	325
INDEX	329

List of Plates

		PAGE
1.	The Deadly "Amanita"	*Frontispiece*
2.	Mycelium, and early vegetation of a mushroom	45
3.	Amanita vernus—development	49
4.	Agaricus (Amanita) muscarius	55
5.	Agaricus campestris	83
6.	Agaricus campestris—various forms of	89
7.	Agaricus gambosus	99
8.	Marasmius oreades. "Fairy-ring"	105
9.	Poisonous Champignons. *M. urens*—*M. peronatus*	111
10.	Agaricus procerus	117
11.	Agaricus (Russula) virescens	123
12.	Edible Russulæ. *R. heterophylla*—*R. alutacea*—*R. lepida*	131
13.	Russula emetica	139
14.	Agaricus ostreatus	145
15.	Agaricus ulmarius	151
16.	Coprinus comatus	157
17.	Coprinus atramentarius	163
18.	Lactarius deliciosus	169
19.	Cantharellus cibarius	175
20.	Boletus edulis	187
21.	Boletus scaber	193

LIST OF PLATES

		PAGE
22.	Edible Boleti. *B. subtomentosus—B. chrysenteron*	199
23.	Strobilomyces strobilaceus	205
24.	Suspicious Boleti. *B. felleus—B. alveolatus*	211
25.	Fistulina hepatica	217
26.	Polyporus sulphureus	225
27.	Hydnum repandum	235
28.	Hydnum caput-medusæ	241
29.	Hydnum caput-medusæ—habitat	243
30.	Clavaria formosa	251
31.	Various forms of Clavaria	253
32.	Morchella esculenta	259
33.	Helvella crispa	265
34.	A group of Puff-balls	271
35.	Spore-surface and spore-print of Agaricus	283
36.	Spore-surface and spore-print of Polyporus (*Boletus*)	285
37.	Spore-print of Amanita muscarius	289
38.	Action of slight draught on spores	291

The Spurned Harvest

"Whole hundred-weights of rich, wholesome diet rotting under the trees; woods teeming with food and not one hand to gather it; and this, perhaps, in the midst of poverty and all manner of privations and public prayers against imminent famine."

C. D. BADHAM

Introduction

A PROMINENT botanical authority connected with one of our universities, upon learning of my intention of perpetrating a popular work on our edible mushrooms and toadstools, was inclined to take issue with me on the wisdom of such publication, giving as his reasons that, owing to the extreme difficulty of imparting exact scientific knowledge to the "general reader," such a work, in its presumably imperfect interpretation by the very individuals it is intended to benefit, would only result, in many instances, in supplanting the popular wholesome distrust of all mushrooms with a rash over-confidence which would tend to increase the labors of the family physician and the coroner. And, to a certain extent, in its appreciation of the difficulty of imparting exact science to the lay mind, his criticism was entirely reasonable, and would certainly apply to any treatise on edible mushrooms for popular circulation which contemplated a too extensive field, involving subtle botanical analysis and nice differentiation between species.

But when we realize the fact—now generally conceded—that most of the fatalities consequent upon mushroom-eating are directly traceable to one particular tempting group of fungi, and that this group is moreover so distinctly marked that a *tyro* could *learn* to distinguish it, might not such a popular work, in its emphasis by careful portraiture and pictorial analysis of this deadly genus—placarding it so clearly and unmistakably as to make it readily recognizable—might not such a work, to that extent at least, accomplish a public service?

Identification of fatal species

Moreover, even the most conservative mycologist will certainly admit that out of the hundred and fifty of our admittedly esculent species of fungi there might be segregated a few which bear such conspicuous characters of outward form and other unique individual features—such as color of spores, gills, and tubes, taste, odor, surface character, color of milky juice, etc.—as to render them easily recognizable even by the " general reader."

Conservative mycology

It is in the positive, affirmative assumption of these premises that the present work is prepared, comprising as it does a selection of a score or more, as it were, self-placarded esculent species of fungi, while putting the reader safely on guard against the fatal species and a few other more or less poisonous or suspicious varieties which remote possibility might confound with them.

Since the publication of a recent magazine article on this topic, and which became the basis of the present elaboration, I have been favored with a numerous and almost continuous correspondence upon mushrooms, including letters from every State in the Union, to say nothing of Canada and New Mexico, evincing the wide-spread interest in the fungus from the gustatory point of view. The cautious tone of most of these letters, in the main from neophyte mycologists, is gratifying in its demonstration of the wisdom of my position in this volume, or, as one of my correspondents puts it, "the frightening of one to death at the outset while extending an invitation to the feast." "Death was often a consequence of toadstool eating," my friend continued, "but I never before realized that it was a *certain* result with *any* particular mushroom, and to the extent of this information I am profoundly thankful."

Popular interest in mushrooms

While, then, from the point of view of desired popularity of my book, the grim greeting of a death's-head upon the frontispiece might be considered as something of a handicap, the author confesses that this attitude is the result of "malice prepense" and deliberation, realizing that he is not offering to the "lay public," for mere intellectual profit, this scientific analysis of certain fungus species. Were this alone the *raison d'être* or the logical outcome of the work —mere *identification* of edible and poisonous species —the grewsome symbol which is so conspicuous on two of my pages might have been spared. But when it is remembered that with the selected list of esculent mushrooms herein offered is implied also an in-

Caution at the threshold

vitation and a recommendation to the feast thereof, with the author as the host—that the digestive functions of his confiding friends or guests are to be made the final arbiters of the correctness of his botanical identification—the ban of bane may as well be pronounced at the threshold. Let the too eager epicurean be "scared to death at the outset," on the general principle *pro bono publico*, and to the conciliation of the author's conscience.

The oft-repeated queries of other correspondents suggest the wisdom of a clearer definition of the limitations of the present work. Several individuals have written in surprise of their discovery of a new toadstool which I "did not include in my pictured magazine list," with accompaniment of more or less inadequate description and somewhat enigmatical sketches, and desiring the name of the species and judgment upon its esculent qualities. Such correspondence is a pleasing tribute to an author, and is herewith gratefully acknowledged as to the past and, with some mental reservations, welcomed as to the future. The number of these communications—occasionally several in a day, and with consequent rapid accumulation—renders it absolutely impossible for a busy man to give them the prompt personal attention which courtesy would dictate. My "mushroom" pigeon-hole, therefore, is still plethoric with the unhonored correspondence of many weeks; and inasmuch as the continual accession more than balances the number of my responses, a fulfilment of my obligations in this direction seems hopeless in contem-

[margin: To correspondents]

INTRODUCTION

plation. I would therefore beg the indulgence of such of my friends as have awaited in vain for my reply to their kind communications, even though the future should bring no tidings from me. All of these letters have been received, and are herewith acknowledged: many of them, too, if I may be pardoned what would seem to be a most ungracious comment, for which the "dead-letter" office would have been the more appropriate destination.

I refer to the correspondence "with accompanying specimens," the letter occasionally enclosed in the same box with the said specimens, **Consider the** which, upon its arrival, arouses a protest **recipient** from the local postal authorities, and calls for a liberal use of disinfectants —a disreputable-looking parcel, which, indeed, would appear more consistently referable to the health-board than to the mycologist. So frequent did this embarrassing episode become that it finally necessitated the establishment of a morgue for the benefit of my mushroom correspondents, or rather for their "specimens," usually accompanied with the queries, "What is the name of this mushroom? Is it edible?" I have been obliged to write to several of my friends that identification of the remains was impossible, that the remnant was more interesting entomologically than botanically, and begging that in the future all such similar tokens shall be forwarded in alcohol or packed in ice.

"First impressions are lasting" and "a word to the wise is sufficient." I would suggest that correspondents hereafter consider the hazard of an introduction under such questionable auspices. Most species of mushrooms are extremely perishable, and their "animal" character, chemically considered, and their tendency to rapid decomposition, render them unfit for transportation for any distance, unless hermetically sealed, or their decay otherwise anticipated.

Rapid decay

In the possibility of a continuance of this correspondence, consequent upon the publication of this present book, the writer, in order to forefend a presumably generous proportion of such correspondence, would here emphasize the fact that he is by no means the authority on mycology, or the science of fungi, which the attitude of his inquiring friends would imply. Indeed, his knowledge of species is quite limited. An early fascination, it is true, was humored with considerable zeal to the accumulation of a portfolio of water-colors and other drawings of various fungi — microscopic, curious, edible, and poisonous — and this collection has been subsequently added to at intervals during his regular professional work.

More than one of the originals of the accompanying colored plates have been hidden in this portfolio for over twenty years, and a larger number for ten or fifteen years, awaiting the further accumulation of that knowledge and experience, especially with reference to the edibility of species, which should warrant the utterance of the long-contemplated book.

The reader will therefore kindly remember that out of the approximate 1000 odd species of fungi entitled by their dimensions to the dignity of "toadstools" or "mushrooms"—after separating the 2000 moulds, mildews, rusts, smuts, blights, yeasts, "mother," and other microscopic species—and out of the 150 recommended edible species, the present work includes only about thirty. This selection has *direct reference to popular utility*, only such species having been included as offer some striking or other individual peculiarity by which they may be simply identified, even without so-called scientific knowledge.

<small>Number of mushroom species</small>

The addition of color to the present list enables its extension somewhat beyond the scope of a series printed only in black and white, as in the distinction of mere form alone an uncolored drawing of a certain species might serve to the popular eye as a common portrait of a number of allied species, possibly including a poisonous variety.

While the study of "fungi" has a host of devotees, the mysteries which involve the origin of life in this great order of the *cryptogamia* having had fascinating attractions to microscopical students and specialists, the study of *economic mycology* has been almost without a champion in the United States. Thus we have many learned treatises on the nature, structure, and habits of fungi—vegetative methods, chemical constituents, specific characters, classification—learned dissertations on the microscopical moulds, mildews, rusts and smuts, blights and ferments, to say nothing of the medico-scientific and awe-inspiring potentialities of the sensational microbe, bacterium

<small>Mycology and mycophagy</small>

bacillus, etc., which are daily bringing humanity within their spell and revolutionizing the science of medicine. But among all the various mycological publications we look in vain for the great desideratum of the practical hand-book on the *economic* fungus—the *mushroom as food!* The mycologist who has been courageous enough to submit his chemical analysis and his botanical knowledge of fungi to the test of esculence in his own being is a *rara avis* among them; indeed, a well-known authority states that "one may number on the fingers of his two hands the entire list of mycophagists in the United States." The absence of such works upon the mushroom and "toadstool," greatly desired for reference at an early period of my career, and little better supplied to-day, led to a resolve of which this volume is but an imperfect fulfilment.

Need of a practical work

The special character of my volume, then—the collateral consideration of the fungus as food—will be sufficient excuse for the omission of a merely technical discourse upon the structure, classification, and vegetation of fungi as a class—a field so fully covered by other authors more competent to discuss these lines of special science, and to a selection of whose works the reader is referred in the list herewith appended, to a number of which I am indebted for occasional quotations. A general idea of the methods of dissemination and habitats of fungi will be found in the final chapter on "spore-prints," while under the discussion of the "Amanita," *Agaricus*

Limitations of this volume

campestris, and the "Fairy Ring" the reader is referred to a condensed account of the methods of vegetation and growth of fungi sufficient for present purposes. Other references of similar character will be noted under "Fungi," in Index.

The most conspicuous disciple of mycophagy—almost the pioneer, indeed, in America—was the late Rev. M. A. Curtis, of North Carolina, whose name heads the bibliography on page 325. For the benefit of those of my readers who may wish to follow the subject further than my pages will lead them, I append the list of edible species of fungi contained in Curtis's Catalogue, each group alphabetically arranged, the esculent qualities of many of which he himself discovered and attested by personal experiment. The favorite habitat of each fungus is also given, and to avoid any possibility of confusion in scientific nomenclature or synonymes, the authority for the scientific name is also given in each instance:

The pioneer American mycophagist

LIST OF EDIBLE AMERICAN MUSHROOMS
FROM THE CATALOGUE OF DR. M. A. CURTIS

Agaricus albellus. De Candolle. Damp woods.
A. (amanita) Cæsarea. Scopoli. In oak forests.
A. (amanita) rubescens. Persoon. Damp woods.
A. (amanita) strobiliformis. Vittadini. Common in woods.
A. amygdalinus. M. A. Curtis. Rich grounds, woods, and lanes.
A. arvensis. Schaeffer. Fields and pastures.
A. bombicinus. Schaeffer. Earth and carious wood.
A. campestris. Linnæus. Fields and pastures.
A. castus. M. A. Curtis. Grassy old fields.
A. cespitosus. M. A. Curtis. Base of stumps.
A. columbetta. Fries. Woods.
A. consociatus. Pine woods.

Agaricus cretaceus. Fries. Earth and wood.
A. esculentus. Jacquin. Dense woods.
A. excoriatus. Fries. Grassy lands.
A. frumentaceous. Bulliard. Pine woods.
A. giganteus. Sowerby. Borders of pine woods.
A. glandulosus. Bulliard. Dead trunks.
A. hypopithyus. M. A. Curtis. Pine logs.
A. mastoideus. Fries. Woods.
A. melleus. Valmy. About stumps and logs.
A. mutabilis. Schaeffer. Trunks.
A. nebularis. Batsch. Damp woods.
A. odorus. Bulliard. Woods.
A. ostreatus. Jacquin. Dead trunks.
A. personatus. M. A. Curtis. Near rotten logs.
A. pometi. Fries. Carious wood.
A. procerus. Scopoli. Woods and fields.
A. prunulus. Scopoli. Damp woods.
A. rachodes. Vittadini. Base of stumps and trees.
A. radicatus. Bulliard. Woods.
A. (russula). Schaeffer. Among leaves in woods.
A. salignus. Persoon. On trunks and stumps.
A. speciosus. Fries. Grassy land.
A. squamosus. Muller. Oak stumps.
A. sylvaticus. Schaeffer. Woods.
A. tessellatus. Bulliard. Pine trunks.
A. ulmarius. Sowerby. Dead trunks.
Boletus bovinus. Linnæus. Pine woods.
B. castaneus. Bulliard. Woods.
B. collinitus. Fries. Pine woods.
B. edulis. Bulliard. Woods.
B. elegans. Fries. Earth in woods.
B. flavidus. Fries. Damp woods.
B. granulatus. Linnæus. Woods and fields.
B. luteus. Linnæus. Pine woods.
B. scaber. Bulliard. Sandy woods.
B. subtomentosus. Linnæus. Earth in woods.
B. versipellis. Fries. Woods.
Bovista nigrescens. Persoon. Grassy fields.
B. plumbea. Persoon. Grassy fields.
Cantharellus cibarius. Fries. Woods.
Clavaria aurea. Schaeffer. Earth in woods.
C. botritis. Persoon. Earth in woods.
C. cristata. Holmskiold. Damp woods.
C. fastigiata. Linnæus. Grassy places.
C. flava. Fries. Earth in woods.
C. formosa. Persoon. Earth in woods.

INTRODUCTION

Clavaria fuliginea. Persoon. Shady woods.
C. macropus. Persoon. Earth.
C. muscoides. Linnæus. Grassy places.
C. pyxidata. Persoon. Rotten woods.
C. rugosa. Bulliard. Damp woods.
C. subtilis. Persoon. Shaded banks.
C. tetragona. Schwartz. Damp woods.
Coprinus atramentarius. Bulliard. Manured ground.
C. comatus. Fries. In stable-yards.
Cortinarius castaneus. Fries. Earth in woods.
C. cinnamomeus. Fries. Earth and wood.
C. violaceus. Fries. Woods.
Fistulina hepatica. Fries. Base of trunks and stumps.
Helvella crispa. Fries. Pine in woods.
H. infula. Schaeffer. Earth and pine logs.
H. lacunosa. Afzelius. Near rotten logs.
H. sulcata. Afzelius. Shady woods.
Hydnum caput-medusæ. Bulliard. Trunks and logs.
H. coralloides. Scopoli. Side of trunks.
H. imbricatum. Linnæus. Earth in woods.
H. laevigatum. Schwartz. Pine woods.
H. repandum. Linnæus. Woods.
H. rufescens. Schaeffer. Woods.
H. subsquamosum. Batsch. Damp woods.
Hygrophorus eburneus. Fries. Woods.
H. pratensis. Fries. Hill-sides.
Lactarius augustissimus. Lasch. Thin woods.
L. deliciosus. Fries. Pine woods.
L. insulsus. Fries. Woods.
L. piperatus. Fries. Dry woods.
L. subdulcis. Fries. Damp grounds.
L. volemus. Fries. Woods.
Lycoperdon bovista. Linnæus. Grassy lands.
Pachyma cocos. Fries. Underground.
Paxillus involutus. Fries. Sandy woods.
Polyporus Berkeleii. Fries. Woods.
P. confluens. Fries. Pine woods.
P. cristatus. Fries. Pine woods.
P. frondorus. Fries. Earth and base of stumps.
P. giganteus. Fries. Base of stumps.
P. leucomelas. Fries. Woods.
P. ovinus. Schaeffer. Earth in woods.
P. poripes. Fries. Wooded ravines.
P. sulphureus. Fries. Trunks and logs.
Marasmius oreades. Fries. Hill-sides.
M. scorodoneus. Fries. Decaying vegetation.

Morchella Caroliniana. Bosc. Earth in woods.
M. esculenta. Persoon. Earth in woods.
Russula alutacea. Fries. Woods.
R. lepida. Fries. Pine woods.
R. virescens. Fries. Woods.
Sparassis crispa. Fries. Earth.
S. laminosa. Fries. Oak logs.
Tremella mesenterica. Retz. On bark.

In the contemplation of such a generous natural larder as the above list implies, Dr. Badham's feeling allusion to the "hundred-weights of wholesome diet rotting under the trees," quoted in one of my earlier illustrated pages, will be readily appreciated.

In the purposely restricted scope of these pages I have omitted a large majority of species in Dr. Curtis's list, known to be equally esculent with those which I have selected, but whose *popular differentiation* might involve too close discrimination and possibly serious error; and while my list is probably not as complete as it might be with perfect safety, the number embraces species, nearly all of them what may be called cosmopolitan types, to be found more or less commonly throughout the whole United States and generally identical with European species. It will be observed that the list of Dr. Curtis is headed by three members of Amanitæ. The particular species cited are well known to be esculent, but they are purposely omitted from my list, which for considerations of safety absolutely excludes the entire genus *Amanita* of the "*poison-cup,*" which is discussed at some length in the succeeding chapter.

For popular utility from the food standpoint my selection presents, to all intents and purposes, a more than sufficient list, the species being easily distinguished, and, with proper consideration to their freshness, entirely safe and of sufficient frequency in their haunts to insure a continually available mushroom harvest throughout the entire fungus season.

The knowledge of their identities once acquired, it is perfectly reasonable to assert that in average weather conditions the fungus-hunter may confine himself to these varieties and still be confronted with an embarrassment of riches, availing himself of three meals a day, with the mere trouble of a ramble through the woods or pastures. Indeed, he may restrict himself to six of these species — the green Russula, Puff-ball, Pasture-mushroom, Campestris (meadow-mushroom), Shaggy-mane, and *Boletus edulis* — and yet become a veritable mycological gourmand if he chooses, never at a loss for an appetizing entrée at his table.

Fungus food always available

In the group of Russulæ and Boleti alone, more than one conservative amateur of the writer's acquaintance finds a sufficient supply to meet all dietary wants.

What a plenteous, spontaneous harvest of delicious feasting annually goes begging in our woods and fields!

A neglected harvest

The sentiment of Dr. Badham, the eminent British authority on mushrooms, years ago, in reference to the spontaneous perennial harvest of wild edible fungi which abounded in his country, going to waste by the ton, would appear to be as true to-day for Britain as when he uttered it, and applies with even greater force to the similar, I may say identical, neglected tribute of Nature in our own American woods and fields, where the growth of fungi is especially rich.

The fungus-eaters of Britain, it is said, are even to-day merely a conspicuous coterie, while in America this particular sort of specialist is more generally an isolated "crank" who is compelled to "flock alone," contemplated with a certain awe by his less venturesome fellows, and otherwise variously considered, either with envy of his experience and scientific knowledge, or more probably as an irresponsible, who continually tempts Providence in his foolhardy experiments with poison.

Fungus epicures

But what a contrast do we find on the Continent in the appreciation of the fungus as an article of diet! In France, Germany, Russia, and Italy, for example, where the woods are scoured for the perennial crop, and where, through centuries of popular familiarity and tradition, the knowledge of its economic value has become the possession of the people, a most important possession to the poor peasant who, perhaps for weeks together, will taste no other animal food. I say "animal food" advisedly; for, gastronomically and chemically considered, the flesh of the mushroom has been proven to be almost identical with meat, and possesses the same nourishing properties. This animal affinity is further suggested in its physiological life, the fungus reversing the order of all

Chemical constituents

other vegetation in imbibing oxygen and exhaling carbonic acid, after the manner of animals. It is not surprising, therefore, that the analogy should be still further emphasized by the discrimination of the palate, many kinds of fungi when cooked simulating the taste and consistency of animal food almost to the point of deception.

But in America the fungus is under the ban, its great majority of harmless or even wholesome edible species having been brought into popular disrepute through the contamination, mostly, of a single small genus. In the absence of special scientific knowledge, or, from our present point of view, its equivalent, popular familiarity, this general distrust of the whole fungus tribe may be, however, considered a beneficent prejudice. So deadly is the insidious, mysterious foe that lurks among the friendly species that it is well for humanity in general that the entire list of fungi should share its odium, else those "toadstool" fatalities, already alarmingly frequent, might become a serious feature in our tables of mortality.

Popular distrust of fungi

But the prejudice is needlessly sweeping. A little so-called knowledge of fungi has often proven to be a "dangerous thing," it is true, but it is quite possible for any one of ordinary intelligence, rightly instructed, to master the discrimination of at least a *few* of the more *common edible* species, while being *thoroughly equipped* against the dangers of *deadly* varieties, whose identification is comparatively simple.

Fungus food for all

It is idle to attempt an adjudication of the vexed "toadstool" and "mushroom" question here. The toad is plainly the only final, appealable authority on this subject. It may be questioned whether he is at pains to determine the delectable or noisome qualities — from the human standpoint — of a particular fungus before deciding to settle his comfortable proportions upon its summit — if, indeed, he even so honors even the humblest of them.

"Toadstool" and "mushroom"

The oft-repeated question, therefore, "Is this fungus a toadstool or a mushroom?" may fittingly be met by the counter query, "Is this rose a flower or a blossom?"

The so-called distinction is a purely arbitrary, popular prejudice which differentiates the "toadstool" as poisonous, the "mushroom" being considered harmless. But even the rustic authorities are rather mixed on the subject, as may be well illustrated by a recent incident in my own experience.

Walking in the woods with a country friend in quest of fungi, we were discussing this "toadstool" topic when we came upon a cluster of mushrooms at the base of a tree-trunk, their broad, expanded caps apparently upholstered in fawn-colored, undressed kid, their under surfaces being stuffed and tufted in pale greenish hue.

Popular discrimination

"What would you call those?" I inquired.

"Those are toadstools, unmistakably," he replied.

"Well, toadstools or not, you see there about two pounds of delicious vegetable meat, for it is the common species of edible boletus—*Boletus edulis*."

A few moments later we paused before a beautiful specimen, lifting its parasol of pure white above the black leaf mould.

"And what is this?" I inquired.

"I would certainly call *that* a mushroom," was his instant reply.

This mushroom proved to be a fine, tempting specimen of the *Agaricus (amanita) vernus*, the deadliest of the mushrooms, and one of the most violent and fatal of all known vegetable poisons, whose attractive graces and insidious wiles are doubtless continually responsible for those numerous fatalities usually dismissed with the epitaph, "Died from eating toadstools in mistake for mushrooms."

So much, therefore, for the popular distinction which makes "toadstool" a synonyme for "poisonous," and "mushroom" synonymous with "edible," and which often proves to be the "little knowledge" which is very dangerous.

The too prevalent mortality traceable to the mushroom is confined to two classes of unfortunates: 1. Those who have not learned that there is such a thing as a fatal mushroom; 2. The provincial authority who can "tell a mushroom" by a number of his so-called infallible "*tests*" or "proofs." There is a large third class to whose conservative caution is to be referred the prevalent arbitrary distinction between "toadstool" and "mushroom," ardent disciples of old Tertullian, who believed in regard to toadstools that "For every different hue they display there is a pain to correspond to it, and just so many modes

The rustic authorities on "mushrooms"

of death as there are distinct species," and whose obstinate dogma, "There is only one mushroom, all the rest are toadstools," has doubtless spared them an occasional untimely grave, for few of this class, from their very conservatism, ever fall victims to the "toadstool."

And what a self-complacent, patronizing, solicitous character this rustic mushroom oracle is! Go where you will in the rural districts and you are sure of him, or perhaps her — usually a conspicuous figure in the neighborhood, the village blacksmith, perhaps, or the simpler "Old Aunt Huldy." Their father and "granther" before them "knew how to tell a mushroom," and this enviable knowledge has been their particular inheritance.

How well we more special students of the fungus know him! and how he wins our tender regard with his keen solicitude for our well-being! We meet him everywhere in our travels, and always with the same old story! We emerge from the wood, perhaps, with our basket brimful of our particular fungus tidbits, topped off with specimens of red Russula and Boletus, and chance to pass him on the road or in the meadow. He scans the basket curiously as he passes us. He has perhaps heard rumors afloat that "there's a city chap in town who is tempting Providence with his foolin' with tudstools;" and with genuine solicitude and superior condescension and awe, all betrayed in his countenance, he must needs pause in his walk to relieve his mind in our behalf. I recall one characteristic episode, of which the above is the prelude.

"Ye ain't a-goin' to eat *them*, air ye?" he asks, anxiously, by way of introduction.

"I am, most certainly," I respond; "that is, if I can get my good farmer's wife to cook them without corning them and inundating them in lemon-juice."

Rustic discrimination

"Waal, then, I'll say good-bye to ye," he responds, with emphasis. "Why, don't ye know them's tudstools, 'n' they'll *kill* ye as *sartin* as *pizen?* I wonder they ain't fetched ye afore this. You never larned tew tell mushrooms. My father et 'em all his life, and so hev I, 'n' I *know* 'em. Come up into my garden yender 'n' I'll show ye haow to tell the *reel mushroom*. There's a lot of 'em thar in the hot-bed naow. Come along. I'll *give* ye a mess on 'em if ye'll only throw them pizen things away."

"And how do you know that those in your garden *are* real mushrooms?" I inquire.

"Why, they ain't *anything* like *them* o' yourn. They're pink and black underneath, and peel up from the edge."

"How many kinds of mushrooms are there, do you suppose?" I ask.

"They's only the *one* kind; all the others is *tudstools* and *pizen*. It's easy to tell the *reel* mushroom. Come up and I'll show ye. Don't eat *them* things, I beg on ye! I vaow they'll *kill* ye!"

At this point he catches a glimpse of a Shaggymane mushroom, which comes to light as I tenderly fondle the specimens, and which is evidently recognized as an acquaintance.

"What!" he exclaims, in pale alarm. "Ye *ain't* goin' t' eat them *too?*"

"Oh yes I am, this very evening," I respond. "I think I'll try them *first*."

"Why, man, yure crazy! You don't know nothin' about 'em. I'd as soon think o' eatin' pizen outright. Them's what we call black-slime tud-stools. They come up out o' manure. I've seen my muck-heap in my barn-yard covered with the nasty things time 'n' ag'in. They look nice 'n' white naow, but they rot into the onsiteliest black mess ye ever see. I know wut I'm sayin'. Ye can't tell me nothin' 'baout *them* tudstools! They keep comin' up along my barn-fence all thro' the fall— *bushels* of 'em."

<small>A rustic authority</small>

"Well, my good friend, it's a great pity, then, that you have not learned something about toadstools as well as mushrooms, for you might have saved many a butcher's bill, and may in the future if you will only take my word that this much-abused specimen is as truly a mushroom as your pink-gilled peeler, and to my mind far more delicious."

"What! Do you mean to tell me thet you have *reely eaten 'em?*"

"Yes, indeed; often. Why, just look at its clean, shaggy cap, its creamy white or pink gills underneath; take a sniff of its pleasant aroma; and here! just taste a little piece—it's as sweet as a nut!" I conclude, offering him the white morsel.

"Not much! I'll make my will first, thank'ee! You let me *see* ye eat a mess of 'em, and if the coroner don't get ye, p'r'aps I'll try on't."

Experiences similar to this one are frequent in the career of every mycophagist, and serve to illustrate the pity and solicitude which he awakens among his fellow-mortals, as well as to emphasize the prevalent superstitions regarding the comparative virtues of the mushroom and toadstool—a prejudice which, by-the-way, in the absence of available popular literature on the subject, and the actual dangers which encompass their popular distinction, is a most beneficent public safeguard.

"Toadstool" prejudice

The mushroom which "he can tell" is generally the *Agaricus campestris*, or one of its several varieties; and knowing this alone, and tempted by no other, this sort of village oracle escapes the fate which often awaits another class, who are not thus conservative, and who extend their definition of mushroom (a word supposed to be synonymous with "edible"), and this mainly through the indorsement of certain so-called infallible tests handed down to them from their forefathers, and by which the esculent varieties may be distinguished from the poisonous. By these so-called "tests" or "proofs" the identification of certain species is gradually acquired. The rural fungus epicure now "knows them by sight," or perhaps has received his information second-hand, and makes his selection without hesitation, with what success may be judged from the incident in my own experience already noted — one which, knowing as I did the frequency and confidence with which my country friend sampled the fungi at his

Popular tests and superstitions

table, filled me with consternation and anxiety for his future.

"How, then, shall we distinguish a mushroom from a toadstool?"

There is no way of distinguishing them, for they are the same.

"How, then, shall we know a poisonous toadstool from a harmless one?" the reader hopelessly exclaims.

This discrimination is by no means as difficult as is popularly supposed, but in the first place, the student must entirely rid himself of all preconceived notions and traditions, such as the following almost world-wide "tests," many of which are easily demonstrated to be worse than worthless, and have doubtless frequently led to an untimely funeral. Some of these are merely local, and in widely separated districts are supplanted by others equally arbitrary and absurd, while many of them are as old as history.

WORTHLESS TRADITIONAL TESTS FOR THE DISCRIMINATION OF POISONOUS AND EDIBLE MUSHROOMS

FAVORABLE SIGNS

1. Pleasant taste and odor.
2. Peeling of the skin of the cap from rim to centre.
3. Pink gills, turning brown in older specimens.
4. The stem easily pulled out of the cap and inserted in it like a parasol handle.
5. Solid stems.
6. Must be gathered in the morning.
7. "Any fungus having a pleasant taste and odor, being found similarly agreeable after being plainly broiled without the least seasoning, is perfectly safe."

INTRODUCTION

UNFAVORABLE SIGNS

8. Boiling with a "silver spoon," the staining of the silver indicating danger.
9. Change of color in the fracture of the fresh mushroom.
10. Slimy or sticky on the top.
11. Having the stems at their sides.
12. Growing in clusters.
13. Found in dark, damp places.
14. Growing on wood, decayed logs, or stumps.
15. Growing on or near manure.
16. Having bright colors.
17. Containing milky juice.
18. Having the gill plates of even length.
19. Melting into black fluid.
20. Biting the tongue or having a bitter or nauseating taste.
21. Changing color by immersion in salt-water, or upon being dusted with salt.

These present but a selection of the more prevalent notions. Taken *in toto*, they would prove entirely safe, as they would practically exclude every species of mushroom or toadstool that grows. But as a rule the village oracle bases his infallibility upon two or three of the above "rules," and inasmuch as the entire list absolutely *omits* the *only* one test by which danger is to be avoided, it is a seven-days' wonder that the grewsome toadstool epitaph is not more frequent.

I once knew an aged dame who was accepted as a village oracle on this as well as other topics, such as divining, palmistry, and fortune-telling, and who ate and dispensed toadstools on a few of the above rules. Strange to say, she lived to a good old age, and no increased mortality is credited to her memory as a result of her generosity.

Absolute worthlessness of above tests

How are these popular notions sustained by the facts? Let us analyze them seriatim and confront each with its refutation, the better to show their entire untrustworthiness.

POPULAR TESTS REFUTED

Pleasant taste and odor (1) is a conspicuous feature in the regular "mushroom" (*Agaricus campestris*), and most other edible fungi, but as a criterion for safety it is a mockery. The deadly *Agaricus amanita*, already mentioned, has an inviting odor and to most people a pleasant taste when raw, and being cooked and eaten gives no token of its fatal resources until from six to twelve hours after, when its unfortunate victim is past hope. (See p. 68.)

Worthless popular tests

The *ready peeling* of the skin (2) is one of the most widely prevalent proofs of probation, and is often considered a *sufficient* test; yet the Amanita will be found to peel with a degree of accommodation which would thus at once settle its claims as a "mushroom." Indeed, a large number of species, including several poisonous kinds, will peel as perfectly as the Campestris.

The pink gills turning brown (3) is a marked characteristic of the "mushroom" (*A. campestris*, Plate 5), and, being a rare tint among the fungus tribe, is really one of the most valuable of the tests, especially as it is limited by rules affecting other pink-gilled species.

The stem being easily pulled out of the cap (4) applies to several edible species, but equally to the poisonous.

The notion that *edible mushrooms have solid stems* (5) would be a very unsafe talisman for us to take to the woods in our search for fungus-food. Many poisonous species are thus solid — the emetic Russula, for example — while the alleged importance of the *morning specimens* (6) is without the slightest foundation.

<small>Worthless popular tests</small>

The passage quoted here (7), or a statement to the same effect, was quite widely circulated in the newspapers a dozen or more years ago, in an article which bore all the indications of authoritative utterance, the assumption being that the poisonous mushroom would invariably give some forbidding token to the senses by which it might be discriminated.

Woe to the fungus epicure who should sample his mushrooms and toadstools on such a criterion as this, as the *most fatal of all mushrooms*, the *Amanita vernus*, would fulfil all these requisites.

The discoloration of silver (8) is a test as old as Pliny at least, a world-wide popular touchstone for the detection of deleterious fungi, but useful only in the fact that it will often exclude a poison not contemplated in the discrimination. On this point, especially as it affords opportunity to emphasize a common disappointment of the mushroom-eater, I quote from a recent work by Julius A. Palmer (see Bibliography, No. 3): "Mushrooms decay very rapidly. In a short time a fair, solid fungus becomes a mass of maggots which eat its tissue until its substance is honey-combed; these cells, on a warm day, are charged with the vapors of decomposition. Now you put such mushrooms as these (and I have seen just such on the markets of Boston and London) over the fire. In boiling, sulphuretted hydrogen or other noxious gases are liberated; you stir with a bright spoon and it is discolored; proud of your test, you throw away your stew. Now this is right, but if from this you conclude that all fungus which discolors silver is poisonous and that which leaves it bright is esculent, you are in dangerous error. It is the same with fish at sea. Tradition says that you must fry a piece of silver with them and throw them away if it discolors. Certainly the experiment does no harm, and shows a decomposition in both cases which might have been detected without the charm." Opposed to this so-called talisman, how grim is the fact that the deadliest of all mushrooms, the Amanita, in its fresh condition, has no effect upon silver.

Worthless popular tests

The change of color in fracture (9) has long been a ban to the fungus as food. But this would exclude several very delicious species, which turn bluish, greenish, and red when broken—viz., *Boletus subtomentosus* (Plate 22), *Boletus strobilaceus* (Plate 23), and Lactarius (Plate 18).

The "toadstools" with "sticky tops" thus discriminated against (10) include a number of esculent species, Boleti and Russulæ, and others, as do also the varieties with side-stems (11)—viz., *Agaricus ulmarius* (Plate 15), *Fistulina hepatica* (Plate 25), *Agaricus ostreatus* (Plate 14), etc.

The clustered fungi (12) have long been included in the black-list without reason, as witness the following esteemed esculent species: The Shaggy-mane (Plate 16), *Coprinus atramentarius* (Plate 17), Oyster mushroom (Plate 14), Elm mushroom (Plate 15), Puff-balls (Plate 34), and Champignon (Plate 8).

Worthless popular tests

To exclude *all fungi which grow in dark, damp places* (13) is a singular inconsistency, as in some localities this would eliminate the very one species of "mushroom" admittedly eatable by popular favor. In many countries these are regularly cultivated for market in dark, damp, subterranean caverns or in cellars. Indeed, the "dark, damp place" would appear to be the ideal habitat of this the "only mushroom!"

Equally absurd is the discrimination against those *growing on wood* (14), which again deprives us of the delicious Hydnum (Plate 27), the Beefsteak (Plate 25), Oyster mushroom (Plate 14), Elm mushroom (Plate 15), and many others, including Puff-balls (Plate 34). If we exclude those growing *upon or near manure* (15), we shall be obliged to omit the Coprinus group (Plates 16 and 17), and often the "*reel* mushroom" as well.

Among the *bright-colored species* (16), it is true, are many dangerous individuals, as, for instance, the deadly Fly Amanita of Plate 4, and the emetic Russula (Plate 13), but on this fiat we should have to reject the other brilliant esculent Russulæ (Plates 11 and 12), the brilliant yellow Chantarelle (Plate 19), the Lactarius (Plate 18), and various other equally palatable and wholesome species.

The objection against *milky mushrooms* (17) would serve to exclude the poisonous species of Lactarius, but would thus include at least two of the delicious species of the group, *L. deliciosus*, with orange milk (Plate 18), and *L. piperatus*, another species with white milk not figured in this volume.

Worthless popular tests

The group of Russulæ, most of which are esculent, is notable for their *gills of even length* (18), though not all the species are thus characterized. This discrimination, however, especially applies to the Shaggy-mane (Plate 16), which is conspicuously even-gilled, and is a decided delicacy.

This species, together with its congener, the edible *Coprinus atramentarius* (Plate 17), are notorious for their *melting into black fluid* (19), which is thus of no significance as a test, although the mushrooms are not supposed to be eaten in this stage of deliquescence.

A fungus which *bites the tongue* (20) when tasted would naturally be excluded from our mushroom diet, as would also, of course, those of a *bitter or nauseating taste;* but several species, notably the *Lactarius piperatus*, as its name implies, is very hot and peppery when raw—a characteristic which disappears in cooking, after which it is perfectly esculent. The same applies in a scarcely less degree to the *Agaricus melleus*, and less so to the *Hydnum repandum* (Plate 27), and other mushrooms. But the poisonous *Russula emetica* (Plate 13) gives this same hot, warning tang, and this rule (17) would at least thus exclude the harmful species, and is thus contributive to popular safety.

The salt test (21), with that of the silver charm, is also a relic of the dim past, but is absolutely useless as a touchstone. Many poisonous spe-
Worthless popular tests cies, notably the Amanita, fail to answer to it. All authorities agree, however, that the addition of salt in cooking, or the preparatory soaking of specimens in brine, has a tendency to render poisonous species innocuous. Indeed, it is claimed that in Russia and elsewhere on the Continent many admittedly poisonous species, even the deadly Fly Amanita, is habitually eaten subsequent to this semi-corning process, by which the poisonous chemical principle is neutralized.

Among this long list, and many other equally arbitrary and ignorant prejudicial traditions, many of which date back to the earliest
Omission of the only true test times, it is indeed astonishing to note the *conspicuous absence* of the one and only valuable sign by which the fatal species could be unmistakably determined—a symbol which was reserved for botanical science to discover: the presence of the "*cup*" in the Amanita, which is pointedly emphasized in my Frontispiece, and the importance of which as a botanical and cautionary distinction is considered at more length in the following chapter.

It is well to consider for a moment what is implied in

"A POISONOUS MUSHROOM"

A fungus may be poisonous in various ways:
1. A distinct and certain deadly poison.

2. The cause of violent digestive or other functional disturbance, but not necessarily fatal.

3. The occasion of more or less serious physical derangement through mere indigestibility.

4. Productive of similar disorders through the employment of decayed or wormy specimens of perfectly esculent species.

5. These same esculent species, even in their fresh condition, may become highly noxious by contact or confinement with specimens of the Amanita by the absorption of its volatile poison, as further described on p. 69.

And lastly comes the question of idiosyncrasy, a consideration which is of course not taken into account in our recommendation of certain well-established food varieties.

Concerning idiosyncrasy

"One man's food another man's poison." The scent of the rose is sometimes a serious affliction, and even the delicious strawberry has repeatedly proven a poison. Even the most wholesome mushroom will occasionally require to be discriminated against, as certain individuals find it necessary to exclude cabbage, milk, onions, and other common food from their diet. When we reflect, moreover, that in its essential chemical affinities the fungus simulates animal flesh, and many of the larger and more solid varieties are similarly subject to speedy decomposition, it is obviously important that *all fungi procured for the table should be collected in their prime, and prepared and served as*

Decaying mushrooms

Fresh specimens

quickly as possible. More than one case of supposed mushroom poisoning could be directly traced to carelessness in this regard, when the species themselves, in their proper condition, had been perfectly wholesome.

There can be no general rule laid down for the discrimination of *an edible fungus.* Each must be *learned* as a species, or at least famil-
<small>No general rule for identification</small> iarized as a kind, even as we learn to recognize certain flowers, trees, or birds.
Within a certain range this discrimination is practised by the merest child. How are the robin, the chippy, and the swallow recognized, or the red clover, and white clover, and yellow clover?

Even in the instances of species which bear a very close outward similarity, how simple, after all, does the distinction become. Here, for in-
<small>Simple botanical discrimination</small> stance, is the wild-lettuce, and its mimic, the *mulgedium*, growing side by side—
to ninety-nine out of a hundred observers *absolutely alike*, and apparently the same species. But how readily are they distinguished, I will not say by the botanist merely, but by any one who will take the small pains of contrasting their specific botanical characters—perfectly infallible, no matter how various the masquerade of their foliage. The lettuce has yellow blossoms, and a seed prolonged into a *long beak*, to whose tip the feathery pappus is attached. The mulgedium has dull bluish flowers, and its pappus is attached to the seed by a hardly perceptible elongation. As with the birds and wild-flowers, so with the fungi: we must learn them as species, even

as we learn to distinguish the difference between the trefoil of the clover and that of the wood-sorrel, or between the innocuous wild-carrot and the poison-hemlock, the harmless stag-horn sumach and its venomous congener, the *Rhus venenata*. There are parallel outward resemblances between esculent and poisonous fungi, but each possesses otherwise its own special features by which it may be identified— variations of gills, pores, spores, taste, odor, color, juice, consistency of pulp, method of decay, etc.

It must not be presumed that the list of edible species just cited from the catalogue of Dr. Curtis includes all the esculents among the fungi. Dr. Harkness has discovered and classified many others. Mr. Palmer and Prof. Charles Peck are never at a loss for their "mess of mushrooms" among their list of nearly a hundred species, while Mr. Charles McIlvaine, whose name, so far as its practical authority is concerned, should appear more prominently in my bibliographical list, but who has not yet incorporated his many mycological essays in book form, writes me that he has tested gastronomically a host of species, and has found over *three hundred* to be edible, or at least harmless. It may be said that the probabilities would include a large majority of the thousand species in the same category. But this is a matter which, in the absence of absolute knowledge, is mere conjecture.

Of the forty-odd species which the writer enjoys with more or less frequency at his table, he is satisfied that he can select at least thirty which possess such distinct and strongly marked characters of form, structure, and other special qualities as to enable them, by the aid of careful portraiture and brief description, to be easily recognized, even by a tyro.

As previously emphasized, the present work does not aim to be complete, nor does it contemplate a practical utility beyond its specific recommendations, nor will the author assume any responsibility for the hazard which shall exceed its restricted list of species.

On general principles, however, considering the proneness of humanity towards the acquisition of forbidden fruit, and reasoning from my own actual experience, and that of many others to whom this fascinating hobby of epicurean fungology has become a growing passion, it may almost be assumed that the fungus appetite with many of my readers will increase by what it feeds on, and the sufficiency herewith offered will scarcely suffice. Like Oliver Twist, they must needs have *more*. The glory of a new acquisition to the fungus menu, and emulation of other rival tyro mycophagists, will doubtless lead many enthusiasts to more or less hazardous experiment among the legion of the unknown species. This logical tendency, then, must be met ere my book can safely and conscientiously be launched upon its career, to which purpose I would append the following condensed

Humanity and forbidden fruit

RULES FOR THE VENTURESOME

1. Avoid every mushroom having a *cup*, or *suggestion* of such, at base (see Frontispiece, and Plates 3 and 4); the distinctly fatal poisons are thus excluded.

2. Exclude those having an unpleasant odor, a peppery, bitter, or other unpalatable flavor, or tough consistency.

3. Exclude those infested with worms, or in advanced age or decay.

4. In testing others which will pass the above probation let the specimen be *kept by itself*, not in contact with or enclosed in the same basket with other species, for reasons given on page 69.

Testing new species Begin by a mere nibble, the size of a pea, and gentle mastication, being careful to swallow no saliva, and finally expelling all from the mouth. If no noticeable results follow, the next trial, with the interval of a day, with the same quantity may permit of a swallow of a little of the juice, the fragments of the fungus expelled as before.

No unpleasantness following for twenty-four hours, the third trial may permit of a similar entire fragment being swallowed, all of these experiments to be made on "an empty stomach." If this introduction of the actual substance of the fungus into the stomach is superseded by no disturbance in twenty-four hours, a larger piece, the size of a hazel-nut, may be attempted, and thus the amount gradually increased day by day until the demonstration of edibility, or at least harmlessness, is complete, and the species thus admitted into the "safe" list. By following this method with the utmost caution the experimenter can at best suffer but a slight temporary indisposition as the result of his hardihood, in the event of a noisome species having been encountered, and will at least thus have the satisfaction of discovery of an enemy if not a friend.

It may be said that any mushroom, *omitting the Amanita*, which is pleasant to the taste and otherwise agreeable as to odor and texture when raw, is probably harmless, and may safely be thus *ventured on* with a view of establishing its edibility. A prominent authority on our edible mushrooms, already mentioned, applies this rule to all the Agarics with confidence.

Mr. McIlvaine's general rule

"This rule may be established," he says: "All Agarics—*excepting the Amanitæ*—mild to the taste when raw, if they commend themselves in other ways, are edible." This claim is borne out in his experience, with the result, already told, that he now numbers over one hundred species among his habitual edible list out of the three hundred which he has actually found by personal test to be edible or harmless. "So numerous are toadstools," he continues, "and so well does a study of them define their habits and habitats, that the writer *never fails upon any day from April to December to find ample supply of healthy, nutritious, delicate toadstools for himself and family*." The italicized portion is my own, as I would thus emphasize the similar possibilities amply afforded even in the present condensed list of about thirty varieties herein described.

In gathering mushrooms one should be supplied with a sharp knife. The mushroom should be carefully cut off an inch or so below the cap, or at least sufficiently far above the ground to escape all signs of dirt on the stem. They should then be laid gills upward in their receptacle, and it is well to have a special basket, arranged with one or two removable bottoms or horizontal partitions, which are kept in place by upright props within, thus relieving the lower layers of mushrooms from the weight of those above them. Such a basket is almost indispensable.

Hints to mushroom= gatherers

Before preparing mushrooms for the table, the specimens should be carefully scrutinized for a class of fungus specialists which we have not taken into account, and which have probably anticipated us. The mushroom is proverbial for its rapid development, but nature has not allowed it thus to escape the usual penalties of lush vegetation, as witness this swarming, squirming host, minute grubs, which occasionally honey-comb or hollow its entire substance ere it has reached its prime; indeed, in many cases, even before it has fully expanded or even protruded above ground.

Insects infesting mushrooms

Like the carrion-flies, the bees, and wasps, which in early times were believed to be of spontaneous origin —flies being generated from putrefaction, bees from dead bulls, and the martial wasps from defunct "war-horses" —these fungus swarms which so speedily reduce a fair specimen of a mushroom to a melting loathsome mass, were also supposed to be the natural progeny of the "poisonous toadstool." But science has solved the riddle of their mysterious omnipresence among the fungi, each particular swarm of grubs being the witness of a former visit of a ma-

History of fungus insects

ternal parent insect, which has sought the budding fungus in its haunts often before it has fully revealed itself to human gaze, and implanted within its substance her hundred or more eggs. To the uneducated eye these larvæ all appear similar, but the specialist in entomology readily distinguishes between them as the young of this or that species of fly, gnat, or beetle.

History of fungus insects

As an illustration of the assiduity with which the history of these tiny scavenger insects has been followed by science, I may mention that in the gnat group alone over seven hundred species have been discovered and scientifically described, many of them requiring a powerful magnifier to reveal their identities.

Specimens of infected or decaying mushrooms preserved within a tightly closed box—and, we would suggest, duly quarantined—will at length reveal the imago forms of the voracious larvæ: generally a swarm of tiny gnats or flies, with an occasional sprinkling of small glossy black beetles, or perhaps a beautiful indigo-blue insect half an inch in length, of most nervous habit, and possessed of a long and very active tail. This insect is an example of the curious group of rove-beetles—*staphylinus*—a family of insect scavengers, many of whose species depend upon the fungi for subsistence.

Even the large woody growth known as "punk" or "touchwood," so frequently seen upon decaying trunks, is not spared. A huge specimen in my keeping was literally reduced to dust by a single species of beetle.

Considering the prevalence of these fungus hosts, it is well in all mushrooms to take the precaution of making a vertical section through stem and cap, excluding such specimens as are conspicuously monopolized, and not being *too* critical of the rest, for the over-fastidious gourmet will often thus have little to show for his morning walk. I have gathered a hundred specimens of fungi in one stroll, perhaps not a quarter of which, upon careful scrutiny, though fair of exterior, would be fit for the table. The fungus-hunter *par excellence* has usually been there before us and left his mark (see page 135)—a mere fine brown streak or tunnel, perhaps, winding through the pulp or stem, where his minute fungoid identity is even yet secreted. But we bigger fungus-eaters gradually learn to accept him — if not too outrageously promiscuous — as a natural part and parcel of our *Hachis aux Champignons*, or our simple mushrooms on toast, even as we wink at the similar lively accessories which sophisticate our delectable raisins, prunes, and figs, to say nothing of prime old Rochefort!

A wise precaution

MUSHROOM POISONING

In conclusion, lest these pages, in spite of the impress of caution with which they are weighted, should lead to discomfiture, distress, or more serious results among their more careless readers, it is well to devote a few lines to directions for medical treatment where such should seem to be required. To this end I quote a passage from an article in the *Therapeutic*

Gazette of May, 1893, from the pen of Mr. McIlvaine, whose many years' experience with gastronomic fungi entitles his words to careful consideration:

<small>Diagnosis and treatment</small>
"The physician called upon to treat a case of toadstool poisoning need not wait to query after the variety eaten; he need not wish to see a sample. His first endeavor should be to ascertain the exact time elapsing between the eating of the toadstools and the first feeling of discomfort. If this is within four or five hours one of the minor poisons is at work, and rapid relief must be given by the administration of an emetic, followed by one or two moderate doses of sweet-oil and whiskey, in equal parts. Vinegar is effective as a substitute for sweet-oil. If from eight to twelve hours have elapsed, the physician may rest assured that amanitine is present, and should administer one-sixtieth of a grain of atropine at once."

This atropine is intended to be injected hypodermically, and the treatment repeated every half-hour until one-twentieth of a grain has been given, or the patient's life saved.

Further consideration of the Amanita and its deadly poison and antidote, with details as to treatment in a notable case, will be reserved for the following chapter.

The colored plates in the volume were prepared from pencil drawings tinted in water-color, many of them direct from nature, several dating back fifteen years, and many of them over twenty years, for their original sketch. The colors as presented indicate those of typical individuals of the various species, and each, in addition to the extended description in the text of the volume, is faced by a condensed description for ready reference, the usual troublesome necessity of turning the pages being thus avoided.

In each plate dimension marks are shown which indicate the expansion of the pileus or cap of the fungus in an ideal specimen.

Acknowledgments

In the preparation of this work, acknowledgments are specially due to Messrs. Julius A. Palmer and Charles McIlvaine for the privilege of liberal quotations from their published works, especially with reference to the poisonous fungi. The volume is also further indebted for occasional extracts from the standard works of Prof. Chas. Peck, Mrs. T. J. Hussey, Rev. Dr. C. D. Badham, Rev. Dr. M. C. Cooke, Rev. J. M. Berkeley, Worthington Smith, and Rev. M. A. Curtis, all of whose volumes and various other contributions on the special subject of mycophagy are included in my bibliography on a later page.

W. HAMILTON GIBSON

October 1, 1894   WASHINGTON, CONN.

The Deadly Amanita

The Deadly Amanita

THE frequency of this terrible foe in all our woods, and the ever-recurring fatalities which are continually traced to its seductive treachery (some twenty-five deaths having been recorded in the public journals during the summer of 1893 alone), render it important that its teeth should be drawn, and its portrait placarded and popularly familiarized as an archenemy of mankind.

As we have seen, from every superficial standpoint, this species is self-commendatory. It is, without doubt, in comeliness, symmetry, and structure, the ideal of all our mushrooms, as it is, indeed, the botanical type of the tribe Agaricus, as well as its most notorious genus. Since the time of that carousing young lunatic Nero, who, doubtless, was wont to make merry with its "convenient poison," upon one occasion, it is recorded by Pliny, to the presumably amusing extinction of the entire guests of a banquet, together with the prefect of the guard and a small host of tribunes and centurions, the Amanita has claimed an army of victims.

A whited sepulchre

While giving no superficial token of its dangerous

character to the casual observer, the Amanita, as a genus and a species, is nevertheless easily identified, if the mushroom collector will for the moment consider it from the *botanical* rather than the sensuous or gustatorial standpoint. The deadly Amanita need no longer impose upon the fastidious feaster in the guise of the dainty "legume" of his menu, or as a contaminating, fatal ingredient in the otherwise wholesome *ragoût*.

Easily identified botanically

In Plate 3 I have presented the reprobate *Amanita vernus* in its protean progressive proportions from infancy to maturity. This is especially desirable, in that the fungus is equally dangerous as an infant, and also because the development of its growth specially emphasizes *botanically* the one important structural character by which the species or genus may be easily distinguished. Let us, then, consider the specimen as a type of the tribe Agaricus (gilled mushroom, see p. 79), genus Amanita.

Amanita vernus

Year after year we are sure of finding this species, or others of the genus, especially in the spring and summer, its favorite haunt being the woods. Its spores, like other mushrooms, are shed upon the ground from the white gills beneath, as described in our chapter on "Spore-prints," or wafted to the ends of the earth on the breeze, and eventually, upon having found a suitable habitat, vegetate in the form of webby, white, mould-like growth — mycelium — which threads through the dead leaves, the earth, or decaying wood. This running growth is botanically considered

PLATE II.—MYCELIUM, AND EARLY VEGETATION OF A MUSHROOM

as the *true* fungus, the final mushroom being the *fruit*, whose function is the dissemination of the spores. After a rain, or when the conditions are otherwise suitable, a certain point among this webby tangle beneath the ground becomes suddenly quickened into astonishing cell-making energy, and a small rounded nodule begins to form, which continues to develop with great rapidity (Plate 2). In a few hours more it has pushed its head above ground, and now appears like an egg, as at A, Plate 3. The successive stages in its development are clearly indicated in the drawings. Each represents an interval of an hour or two, or more, the most suggestive and important feature being the *outer envelope*, or *volva*, which encloses the actual mushroom — at first completely, then in a ruptured condition, until in the mature growth the only vestige of it which appears above ground are the few shreds generally, though not always, to be seen on the top of the cap. The *most important* character of this deadly Amanita is, therefore, apparently with almost artful malice prepense, often *concealed* from our view in the mature specimen, the only remnant of the original outer sack being the *cup* or *socket* about the base of the stem, which is generally hidden under ground, and usually there remains after we pluck the specimen.

Vegetation of an Agaric

The danger signal

This "poison-cup" may be taken as the cautionary symbol of the genus Amanita, common to all the species. *Any mushroom or toadstool, therefore, whose stem is thus set in a socket, or which has any suggestion of such a socket, should be labelled "poison";* for, though some of the species having this cup are edible, from the popular point of view, it is wiser and certainly safer to condemn the entire group. But the cup must be *sought* for. We shall thus at least avoid the possible danger of a fatal termination to our amateur experiments in gustatory mycology; for, while various other mushrooms might, and do, induce even serious illness through digestive disturbance, and secondary, possibly fatal, complications, the Amanita group are now conceded to be the only fungi which contain a positive, active poisonous principle whose certain logical consequence is death.

The poison=cup

Another structural feature of the Amanita is shown in the illustration, but has been omitted from the above consideration to avoid confusion. This is the "veil" which, in the young mushroom, originally connected the edge of the cap, or pileus, with the stem, and whose gradual rupture necessarily follows the expansion of the cap, until a mere frill or ring is left about the stem at the original point of contact.

The "veil" or shroud

But this feature is a frequent character in many edible mushrooms, as witness the several examples in the edible species of our plates, and therefore of no dangerous significance *per se*, being merely a membrane which protects the growing gills.

Nor are the other features, the remnants of the volva on the summit of the cap, to be considered of primary importance from the popular point of view, for the reason—firstly, that these fragments, while con-

PLATE III.—DEVELOPMENT OF AMANITA VERNUS

spicuous and constant in *Amanita muscarius* (Plate 4), are *not* thus permanent in several other species of Amanitæ, notably the white-satin-capped *Amanita vernus*, *Amanita phalloides*, and *Amanita Cæsarea*, in which the fragments are deciduous; and, secondly, because the same general effect of these warty scales is so clearly imitated in other mushrooms which are distinctly edible, as in examples Plate 10 and Plate 16. It is to the *volva* or *cup*, then, that we must devote our special attention as the only safe and constant character. And this leads me to the prominent and necessary consideration of another common species of Amanita, mentioned above, in which even this cup is more or less obscure.

Scales and scurfy spots

THE POISONOUS FLY-MUSHROOM
Agaricus (Amanita) muscarius

This, one of the most strikingly beautiful of our toadstools, is figured in Plate 4. Its brilliant cap of yellow, orange, or even scarlet, studded with white or grayish raised spots, can hardly be unfamiliar to even the least observant country walker. Its favorite habitat is the woods, and, in the writer's experience especially, beneath hemlocks and poplars, where he has seen this species year after year in whole companies, and in all stages shown in the plate at the same time, from the globular young specimen almost covered with its white warts just lifting its head above the brown carpet to the fully expanded

A deceptive Amanita

individual, in which the spots have assumed a shrunken and brownish tint.

The consideration of this species is of the *utmost importance*, as its beauty is but an alluring mask, which has enticed many to their destruction; among the more recent of its conspicuous victims having been the Czar Alexis of Russia. For this is another cosmopolitan type of mushroom, common alike in America, Great Britain, Europe, and Asia, in all of which countries it is notorious for its poisonous resources. It is commonly known as the " Fly-agaric," its substance macerated in milk having been employed for centuries as an effectual fly-poison. After the reader's introduction to the botanical character of the Amanita, he would, presumably, be somewhat suspicious of the present species. The suggestive white or dingy fragments upon its cap, it is true, would alone arouse his suspicions, but in the examination of the stem for the telltale volva or cup its verification might be somewhat in doubt. It is for this reason that the species is emphasized in these pages, as the *Amanita muscarius*, judging from the great dissimilarity of its numerous portraits from all countries, would seem to be remarkably protean, especially with reference to its stalk. The majority of the portraits of this reprobate presents the volva as distinct and as clean cut as in the *A. vernus* just described, and the stalk above as equally smooth, features which are usually at variance with the associated botanical description of the species, which

margin notes: Used as a fly-poison; Its obscure cup

Amanita muscaria

PLATE IV

FLY MUSHROOM

Agaricus (Amanita) muscarius

Pileus: Diameter three to six inches, quite flat at maturity; color brilliant yellow, orange, or scarlet, becoming pale with age, dotted with adhesive white, at length pale brownish warts, the remnants of the volva.

Gills: Pure white, very symmetrical, various in length, the shorter ones terminating under the cap with an almost vertical abruptness.

Spores: Pure white. A spore-print of this species is shown in Plate 37.

Stem: White, yellowish with age, becoming shaggy, at length scaly, the scales below appearing to merge into the form of an obscure cup.

Volva: Often obscure, indicated by a mere ragged line of loose outward curved shaggy scales around a bulbous base.

Flesh: White.

Habitat: Woods and their borders, especially favoring pine and hemlock.

Season: Summer and autumn.

AMANITA MUSCARIA. (POISONOUS.)

PLATE IV

often characterizes the volva as "incomplete" or "obscure," and the stem as "rough and scaly." If the portraits in these works are correct, the Amanita qualities of the species are clearly displayed, but if their accompanying descriptions are to be credited, and such seem to be in perfect accord with the specimens which I have always found, the *A. muscarius* would seem in need of a more authentic historian.

The example figured in the plate presents the stem and volva as they have always appeared in specimens obtained by the writer. In the young individuals the stem is waxy-white, becoming later a dull, pale ochre hue, the lower half being shaggy and torn, and beset with loose projecting woolly points which resolve themselves below into scales with loose tips curved outward, and so distantly disposed upon the bulbous base as to leave *no marked definition* of the continuous rim or opening of a cup. But the cup is there, and in a section of the bud state of the mushroom could have been seen, even as in the *white warts* upon the surface of the *younger* specimens we note the evidences of the upper portion of the same white *volva*. In many other species of Amanita, notably *A. vernus*, as already mentioned, these volva fragments generally wither and are shed from the cap. They are thus not to be counted on as a permanent token. But in the fly-mushroom they form a *distinct character*, as they *adhere firmly to the smooth skin* of the pileus, and in drying, instead of shrivelling and curling and falling off, simply shrink, turn brownish, and in the maturely expanded

<small>Volva scales permanent</small>

mushroom appear like scattered drops of mud which have dried upon the pileus. Another peculiar structural feature of this mushroom is shown in the sectional drawing herewith given. The shorter gills, instead of rounding off as they approach the pileus

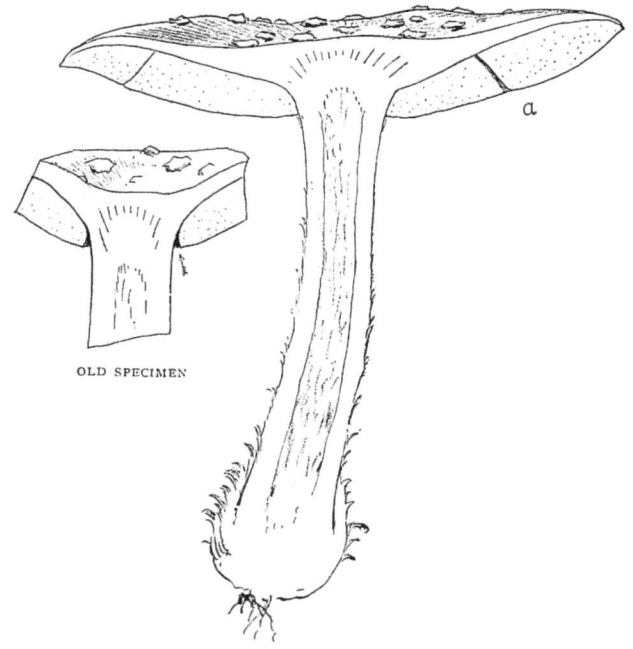

OLD SPECIMEN

SECTION OF FLY-AMANITA

(see *a*), terminate abruptly almost at right angles to their edge. The contrast from the usual form will be more apparent by comparison with the section of the parasol-mushroom on page 114.

Few species of mushrooms have such an interesting history as this. Its deadly properties were known to the ancients. From the earliest times its deeds of notoriety are on record.

This is quite possibly the species alluded to by Pliny as "very conveniently adapted for poisoning," and is not improbably the mushroom referred to by this historian in the following quotation from his famous *Natural History:* " Mushrooms are a dainty food, but deservedly held in disesteem since the notorious crime committed by Agrippina, who through their agency poisoned her husband, the Emperor Claudius; and at the same moment, in the person of her son Nero, inflicted another poisonous curse upon the whole world, herself in particular."

<small>Historical Amanita</small>

Notwithstanding its fatal character, this mushroom, it is said, is habitually eaten by certain peoples, to whom the poison simply acts as an intoxicant. Indeed, it is customarily thus employed as a narcotic and an exhilarant in Kamchatka and Asiatic Russia generally, where the Amanita drunkard supplants the opium fiend and alcohol dipsomaniac of other countries. Its narcotizing qualities are commemorated by Cooke in his *Seven Sisters of Sleep*, wherein may be found a full description of the toxic employment of the fungus.

<small>Amanita dipsomaniacs</small>

The writer has heard it claimed that this species of Amanita has been eaten with impunity by certain individuals; but the information has usually come from sources which warrant the belief that another harmless species has been confounded with it. The warning of my Frontispiece may safely be extended to the fly-amanita. Its beautiful gossamer veil may aptly symbolize a shroud.

By fixing these simple structural features of the Amanita in mind, and emphasizing them by a study of our Frontispiece, we may now consider ourselves armed against our greatest foe, and may with some assurance make our limited selection among this lavish larder of wild provender continually going to waste by the ton in our woods and pastures and lawns. For it is now a fact generally believed by fungologists, and being gradually demonstrated, that the edible species, far from being the exception, as formerly regarded, are the rule; that a great majority of our common wild fungi are at least harmless, if not positively wholesome and nutritious as food.

Forewarned and forearmed

THE POISONOUS ALKALOID

The toxic and deadly effects of certain mushroom poisons, as already described, have been known since ancient times; and the prolonged intoxicating debauches to-day prevalent among the Amanita dipsomaniacs of Northern Russia and Kamchatka, consequent upon the allurements of the decoction of the fly-agaric, are well-known matters of history.

The true chemical character of this poison, however, was not discovered until 1868, when it was successfully isolated by chemical analyses of Drs. Vigier, Schmiedeberg, Currie, and Koppe, and ascertained to be an alkaloid principle, to which was given originally the name of bulbosine, since variously known as muscarine, and finally and most appropriately amanitine.

The poison thus identified, it was reserved to an American authority on edible fungi, Mr. Julius A. Palmer, of Boston, to discover the fact **Mr. Palmer's discovery** of its confinement to but one fungus family — the Amanita.

In the year 1879, in an article contributed by him to the *Moniteur Scientifique*, of Paris, he states:

"Mushrooms are unfit for food by decay or other cause, producing simply a disagreement with the system by containing some bitter, acrid, or slimy element, *or by the presence of a wonderful and dangerous alkaloid which is absorbed in the intestinal canal.* This alkaloid, so far as known, is *found only in the Amanita family.*"

To Mr. Palmer, then, is due the chemical segregation of the Amanita group as the only repository of this deadly toxic.

It has not been discerned in other species of fungi, whose so-called "poisonous" effects are more often traceable to mere indigestibility, the **Lesser poisoning** selection of "over-ripe" specimens, or to idiosyncrasy, rather than to their distinctly poisonous properties.

Many mushrooms of other families which *do* possess ingredients chemically at war with the human system — as the *Russula emetica* and certain *Lactarii*, for instance — at least give a fair warning, either by taste or odor, of their dark intentions.

Owing to the numerous deaths every year consequent upon mushroom-eating, and nearly always directly traceable to the Amanita, the discovery of an antidote to this poison has been the quest of many noted chemists — several supposed antidotes having been experimented with upon dogs and other animals without desired results. These included atropine, the deadly crystalline alkaloid from the *Atropa belladonna*. The earlier experiments upon animals with this drug in Paris, as described by Dr. Gautier in 1884, while encouraging, were not considered conclusive, but were sufficient to warrant the suggestion that the treatment upon man might be effective. In a résumé of the subject in the Philadelphia *Medical and Surgical Reporter*, December, 1885, for the benefit of the medical practitioners who are so frequently called upon to attend cases of mushroom poisoning, Captain Charles McIlvaine recommended the administration of a dose of atropine of from 0.05 to 0.0002 milligramme, and it was later reserved for the same gentleman to witness the first authentic instance of the application of this remedy in antagonism with the Amanita poison in the human system. The report of this experience was afterwards published (see Bibliography, No. 6), embodying also a complete and authentic account of the symptoms and treatment of the cases by the attending physician, Dr. J. E. Shadle, of Shenandoah, Pa., which account I feel is appropriately included here, being in full sympathy with the solicitous spirit of my pages. I therefore quote the statement of Dr. Shadle for the benefit of those interested.

SHENANDOAH, PA., October 26, 1885.

Mr. CHAS. McILVAINE :

MY DEAR SIR,—In compliance with your request, I take pleasure in submitting to your consideration the following report of five cases of toadstool-poisoning which recently came under my observation and treatment:

On Monday, August 31, at 10 A.M., I was hastily called to see a family, consisting of Mr. F., his wife, his mother-in-law, Mrs. R., and his brother-in-law, Thomas R., who, the messenger stated, were having "cramps in the bowels."

Amanita poisoning symptoms

Promptly responding to the call, I found them suffering from intense abdominal pains, nausea, vomiting, boneache, and feelings of distress in the *præcordial* region.

Mr. F., twenty-nine years of age, was a miner by occupation, and had led an intemperate life. Mrs. F., twenty-two years of age, was a brunette, possessing a delicate body, and bearing a decided *neurotic* tendency. Mrs. R., forty-five years of age, was a small *nervo-bilious* woman. Thomas R., thirteen years of age, was a youth well developed.

While I was examining these patients, Mrs. B., forty years of age, a neighbor of the family, presented herself, manifesting in a milder degree the same symptoms. She was a tall, spare woman. Previous to their present attack of illness their general health was good; in none could signs of disease be traced.

Picture to your mind five persons suffering from cholera morbus in its most aggravated form, and you will be enabled to form a pretty correct idea of what I beheld in the Faris residence on Monday morning, August 31.

That five individuals, four being members of one household, should be attacked simultaneously by a similar train of symptoms, naturally gave rise in my mind to a suspicion that something poisonous had been eaten. Upon close inquiry I obtained the following history:

On the afternoon of Sunday, August 30, Mr. F. and Thomas R. were walking through a wood not far distant from their home, and, in wandering from place to place, found clusters of very beautiful toadstools growing abundantly under trees, among which the chestnut predominated.

Attracted by their appearance, and supposing them to be edible, they gathered a large quantity, with the anticipation of having a delicious dish for their Sunday evening meal.

Amanita poisoning symptoms

Various other kinds were growing in the same locality, but this particular variety impressed them as being the most inviting. A correct specimen of the *fungus* they had collected having been sent you, I will leave its botanical description to your pen.

At about nine o'clock, five hours after gathering them, Mrs. F. cooked three pints of the toadstools, stewing them in milk, and seasoning with butter, pepper, and salt.

They had dinner at a very early hour on this day, and by the time they had supper all felt exceedingly hungry, in consequence of which they ate quite heartily. Mrs. F. and her brother vied with each other as to the quantity they could eat. In addition to this dish, bread and butter and coffee were served.

Soon after supper the family retired. None experienced the least discomfort until towards daybreak, when considerable distress in the abdominal organs and cerebral disturbance manifested themselves. Prominent among the initial symptoms were foul breath, coated tongue, pain in the stomach, nausea, and a peculiar sickening sensation in the epigastrium. These symptoms gradually increased in severity, and in twelve hours after the ingestion of the poison, when I made my first visit, the condition of the victims involved great danger. Intense vomiting was present in four, while in Mrs. R.'s case a violent retching seemed to persist.

Gastro-intestinal irritation, followed by a relaxed condition of the bowels, showed itself in about thirty hours after the onset of the more active symptoms. With the appearance of this trouble an insufferable tenesmus developed, producing paroxysms of severe agony. This was particularly true in the case of Mrs. R., whose suffering was so great that it became a formidable symptom to combat. Upon the subsidence of the more severe symptoms, the patients fell into a state of extreme prostration, accompanied by stupor and cold extremities. In the mother, son, and daughter this was profoundly marked. They were completely indifferent to persons and things around them, as well as to their own suffering.

As the symptoms increased in violence, Thos. R. advanced into a state of coma, and Mrs. F. into coma vigil, and remained so for about twelve hours prior to death. The face had a shrunken and wrinkled appearance, the eyes were sunken, the skin was dusky, and the surface of the body was dry and cold to the touch. The pulse, a number of hours before death, was imperceptible at the wrist, and the heart-sounds were scarcely perceived by auscultation.

<small>Amanita poisoning symptoms</small>

The pulse in all cases was notably affected, ranging from 120 to 140 per minute. In character it was soft and compressible; intermittent at intervals.

There was a distinct rise of temperature; the thermometer in the axilla registered as much as 140° F.

A mild form of delirium was an occasional event. In the case of Mrs. F. it formed an important element.

Respecting the special senses, it is well to mention that sight was peculiarly affected. Notwithstanding the fact that the pupils responded kindly to the action of the light, an unpleasant sensation of blindness frequently appeared, and continued for a few minutes.

In spite of all that was done to counteract its ravages, the effects of the poison were so extremely deadly that a fatal issue was the result in two cases. Thomas R. died in fifty-six and Mrs. F. in sixty-three hours after the ingestion of the toadstools.

Treatment.—The treatment instituted was mainly symptomatic.

Fearing that undigested particles of toadstools might still be lying in the gastro-intestinal tract, to Mrs. R., who had not freely vomited, an emetic was administered, and to the rest a mild purge.

<small>Amanita poisoning treatment</small>

An intense thirst and a burning sensation being present in the mouth, throat, and stomach, small pieces of cracked ice were freely used with a view to allaying it.

For the gastro-intestinal irritation I prescribed with satisfactory results the following:

℞ Bismuth subnit., ʒv ;
 Creosote, gtt. xv ;
 Mucil. acaciæ, f℥i ;
 Aq. menth. pip., q.s. ad f℥iii. M.
 Sig.—Teaspoonful every one or two hours.

$1/8$ grain of morph. sulph. was administered hypodermically to alleviate as much as possible the abdominal suffering.

The impending exhaustion and the failing heart's action I endeavored to combat with a free administration of alcoholic stimulants in combination with moderate doses of tincture of digitalis both by the mouth and under the skin.

In order to invite the circulation of the blood to the ice-cold surface of the body, heated bricks and bottles filled with hot water were placed in bed around the patients.

Analyzing each symptom as it arose, and carefully observing the effects of the poison on the system, I formed the opinion that the toxic element contained in the noxious fungus eaten by these people was narcotic in its nature and spent its force on the nerve centres, especially selecting the one governing the function of respiration and the action of the heart.

Diagnosis

Acting upon this conclusion, I began, in the early part of my treatment, subcutaneous injections of sulphate of atropine in frequently-repeated doses, ranging from $\frac{1}{180}$ to $\frac{1}{90}$ grain. The injections invariably were followed by a perceptible improvement in the patient; the heart's action became stronger, the pulse returned at the wrist, and the respiration increased in depth and fulness.

Through the agency of this remedy, supported by the other measures adopted, three (or sixty per cent.) of the patients recovered.

The lessons I draw from this experience are :

1. The poisoning produced by this variety of toadstool is slow in manifesting its effects.

2. That it destroys life by a process of asthenia.

3. That in atropine we have an antidote, and it should be pushed heroically from the earliest inception of the action of the poison.

I have the honor to remain

Yours very respectfully,

J. E. SHADLE, M.D.

In reply to the queries, Was atropine administered in all the cases? and What was the total amount administered to each? Dr. Shadle responded as follows:

SHENANDOAH, PA., October 29, 1885.

MY DEAR MR. MCILVAINE:

Yours of the 27th I have received. The two questions you ask me therein I see are very important, and they should be answered as fully as possible. I am sorry I overlooked the matter in my report.

Before attempting an answer, it is well for me to note right here that Mrs. B., the neighbor, did not eat very much of the toadstool stew; Mrs. R. and Mr. F. each ate about the same quantity — from one and one-half to two platefuls. This is according to Faris's statement. But the two fatal cases— Thomas R. and Mrs. F.— tried to see which could eat the most, and consequently got their full share of the poison. The cat mentioned before had about a tablespoonful of the broth, and they tell me she was very sick. Whether or not she died is not known.

Amanitine and atropine

Now as to the treatment by atropine, I think I can approximate a pretty correct statement in reply to your queries. Not knowing that atropine was considered an antidote, I began its employment in the treatment of these cases from the physiological knowledge I had of the drug relative to its action in other diseases in which there was heart-failure and embarrassed respiration.

When I saw the U. S. Dispensatory suggested it, I of course felt it my duty to use it, as I could find nowhere anything else mentioned as an antidote. I feel convinced that it was by means of the atropine that I saved three of the five patients. Why do I think so? Because whenever I would administer the remedy the patient rallied, the pulse returned at the wrist, the heart-sounds became stronger, and the respiration increased in strength and fulness. What more conclusive evidence do I want than this to show as to how the agent was acting?

When I first saw the patients—twelve hours after the ingestion of the poison—their symptoms were alike, one suffering as much as the other (August 31). I began the use of the alkaloid in the evening of the same day, when I saw the powers of life giving way, the heart failing, and the respiration becoming shallow. It was used in all the cases as follows :

Administration of antidote

Mrs. B., $\frac{1}{180}$, $\frac{1}{90}$, $\frac{1}{90}$, or $\frac{5}{180}$, or $\frac{1}{30}$ gr.
Mr. F., $\frac{1}{180}$, $\frac{1}{90}$, $\frac{1}{90}$, $\frac{1}{90}$, or $\frac{7}{180}$ gr.
Mrs. R., $\frac{1}{180}$, $\frac{1}{90}$, $\frac{1}{90}$, $\frac{1}{90}$, or $\frac{7}{180}$ gr.
Thos. R., $\frac{1}{180}$, $\frac{1}{90}$, $\frac{1}{90}$, $\frac{1}{90}$, $\frac{1}{90}$, or $\frac{9}{180}$, or $\frac{1}{20}$ gr.
Mrs. F., $\frac{1}{180}$, $\frac{1}{90}$, $\frac{1}{90}$, $\frac{1}{90}$, $\frac{1}{90}$, or $\frac{9}{180}$, or $\frac{1}{20}$ gr.

In accordance with the above formulæ the drug was administered. I visited the patients at intervals of six or eight hours, and at each visitation they received an injection in the doses above mentioned. From this we see that in all Mrs. B. received gr. $\frac{1}{30}$ of atropine; Mr. F. received gr. $\frac{7}{180}$ of atropine; Mrs. R. received gr. $\frac{7}{180}$ of atropine; Thos R. (fatal) received gr. $\frac{1}{20}$ of atropine; Mrs. F. (fatal) received gr. $\frac{1}{20}$ of atropine.

The alkaloid failing to save the two that died I think can be attributed to one of two causes, or probably both :

1. That the use of atropine was begun too late and not used heroically enough.

2. That so much of the poison was taken up by the system in these cases that it became too virulent to counteract.

From the history of the cases I know they ate by far the largest quantity. My opinion leans towards the first probable cause I have mentioned.

Another fact worth stating here is that the pupils never became affected by the administration of these doses.

Hoping this will make the matter satisfactory, I remain

Yours truly, J. E. SHADLE.

The interval between the ingestion and the symptoms is, therefore, a most important aid in the diagnosis of a case of mushroom poisoning; and in the event of an Amanita, heretofore absolutely fatal, it is presumably under the control of medical science, now that the deadly toxic principle has at last found its enemy in the neutralizing properties of the equally deadly atropine.

It would seem, moreover, from the severe personal experience of Mr. Julius A. Palmer, that the poison of the Amanita is quite capable of mischief without being taken into the digestive organs. So volatile is this dangerous alkaloid that it may produce violent effects upon the system either through its odor alone, or by simple contact with the skin and consequent absorption.

Mr. Palmer, in his before-mentioned article in the *Moniteur Scientifique*, Paris, relates the following experiences:

"Once while perspiring from a long walk I undertook to bring in a large bunch of the Amanita for an artist. Seated in a close car, holding them in my warm hand, although protected by a paper wrapper, a fearful nausea overcame me. The toadstool was not at first suspected, yet I had all the symptoms of a sea-sick person, and was only relieved by a wide distance between myself and the exciting cause.

Poisons by contact and odor

"While writing this article," he continues, "a friend sent me two very elegant specimens of the Amanita tribe. They were in a confined box. On opening it I smelled of them a few times, and allowed the box to lie near my desk while I wrote to a medical gentleman anxious to procure such for chemical experiment. Having sent them away the matter was dismissed from my mind for three hours after, when, by an attack of vomiting and oppression at the stomach, they were enforced upon my attention. The whites of my eyes became livid, and even until noon the day following the leaden color of my face was noticed by more than one person."

The moral of this story is that the less the reader has to do with Amanita fungi the better. Let them have a wide berth, or at most an an-
<small>A wide berth to Amanita</small> nihilating kick, lest by their alluring beauty they tempt the next unwary traveller who shall encounter them.

But you desire a specimen "to show a friend," or "to make a photograph of, or a sketch," perhaps. In such case it were well to consider further the experiences of Mr. Palmer, which will show the wisdom of keeping your gustatorial and artistic mycology in separate expeditions, or at least of providing your poison-exhaling Amanita specimen with a cage by itself. In the same article he continues:

" Mushrooms make the same use of the atmosphere as men, even their exhalations are accordingly vitiated with their properties. Those not
<small>Mushrooms inoculated by contact</small> deadly thus attack humanity—namely, by absorption of their essential elements by the whole system. They also *inoculate each other* with or without contact, so that *if edible and noxious toadstools are gathered together the former will absorb the properties of the latter.*"

In proof of this assertion he instances a personal experience as follows: " About four years ago a number of poisonous mushrooms (not Amanitæ, but of a totally different family) were sent me with edible fungus. The two varieties had lain twelve hours in the same box. The noxious ones were rejected, and the esculent washed and eaten. In a moment my appetite was gone; violent perspiration, vertigo, and trembling were the next symptoms; then chills, nausea, purging, and tenesmus, all within thirty minutes. Now the substance could not have reached the intestines. The virus absorbed from the noxious fungus permeated the whole system through eating the harmless ones; unmixed with other food it acted upon the muscles through an empty stomach; once spent, the ailment passed off," etc.

From these and other experiences he draws the following conclusions: The poisonous principle of a fungus being absorbed by a harmless element, if the latter be eaten the venom acts more quickly. In reinforcement of this he states that "if the Amanita be cut in sections and laid in vinegar the fungus may be eaten without danger to life; but on a very small dose of the vinegar, death will follow more speedily than if the whole toadstool be eaten." Further interesting matter upon this topic is contained in the article from which I quote, and to which the reader is referred in his volume included in my bibliographical list. The work also contains numerous other collected articles of Mr. Palmer's upon this subject of fungi, to which he has devoted so much attention, and with which his name has become so popularly identified in America.

Poison extracted by vinegar

The allusion to vinegar as an absorbent of the poison suggests the prevalent habitual use of salt as a safeguard by many in the employment of the fungus as food, as both of these ingredients play a prominent part in a fungus cuisine. It is averred by some writers that one of the most noxious of Amanitæ—the Fly-agaric—is eaten in some countries, notably Russia, without unpleasant results, while it is confidently asserted to be harmless after, as it were, having its venom drawn by a soaking in brine previous to cooking. Boiling—both in the possible neutralizing of the poison through heat, and in the withdrawal of the same in the solution—would also be contributive to safety in such cases, provided the tainted liquid were not retained as in a stew or soup.

Effect of salt and heat

On this topic it is interesting to note the epicurean perversity of a certain French author, who, in the face of the already overwhelming abundance of nature's esculent species of fungi, must needs include all the deadly Amanitæ as well, though he gives a recipe by which the poison is extracted by the copious aid of salt, vinegar, boiling water, and drawing. This process, on general principles, might invite humorous speculation as to the appetizing qualities of the residual morsel thus acquired, or as to the advisability of deliberately selecting a poisonous substance for the desideratum of the washed-out, corned, spiced, nondescript remnant which survives the process of extraction, not only of its noxious properties, but of even what nutriment it might possibly contain.

Epicurean perversity

Fancy a beefsteak similarly " prepared," all its nourishing ingredients extracted and thrown away; its exhausted remnant of muscular fibre now the mere absorbent vehicle for vinegar, salt, lemon-juice, butter, nutmeg, garlic, spice, cloves, and other seeming indispensables to the preparation of the Champignon *à la mode!*

<small>Mushrooms à la mode</small>

The verdict of the extreme fungus epicure upon the delectable flavor of this or that mushroom must indeed be taken *cum grano salis*, the customary culinary treatment, or maltreatment, of these delicately flavored fruits having for its apparent object the elimination as far as possible of any suggestion of the true flavor of the fungus. I fancy that even the caustic, rebellious root of the Indian-turnip or the skunk-cabbage thus tamed and subdued in a smothering emollient of spiced gravy or ragoût might negatively serve a purpose as more or less indigestible pabulum.

While, as already mentioned, a few of this genus Amanita are edible, it is well in concluding our chapter to emphasize the caution of an earlier page as to the absolute exclusion of the entire genus from the bill of fare of the amateur mycophagist.

<small>Enough without Amanita</small>

There is an abundance of wholesome, delicious fungi at our doors without them.

Many species of Amanita are to be found more or less frequently in company with the esculent varieties recommended in the chapters following. Among these the two extremes of variation from the typical form are seen in the *A. muscarius* in its permanent retention of the volva scales and the obscurity of its cup, and in the *A. phalloides*, herewith pictured about half natural size, with the frequent *entire absence* of

74   EDIBLE MUSHROOMS

these remnant scales, which wither and fall off, leaving the yellowish or greenish cap perfectly smooth.

It is to the *volva* or *cup*, then, that we must turn for the one fixed permanent character by which this genus is to be identified.

AMANITA PHALLOIDES

UR introductory description of the Amanita presents the most perfect botanical type of a large division of the fungus tribe, the *Agaricaceæ*, or gill-bearing mushrooms, one of the two great orders of fungi which include the large majority of edible species.

A brief consideration of the general classification of fungi will not be out of place at the head of this chapter.

CLASSIFICATION OF FUNGI

A fungus is a cellular cryptogamous (flowerless) plant, nourished through its spawn or mycelium in place of roots, living in air, and propagated by spores.

Fungi—*mycetes*—are naturally subdivided into two great divisions:

1. SPORIFERA—those in which the spores or reproductive bodies are *naked* or soon exposed, as shown in illustration on page 79.

2. SPORIDIIFERA—in which the spores are *enveloped* in sacs or *asci*. These resemble in shape the *cystidium* of illustration on page 79.

The first of these divisions — the SPORIFERA, or naked-spored fungi — is again subdivided into four families, as follows:

1. *Hymenomycetes.* Hymenium, or spore-bearing surface, *exposed* and conspicuous, as seen in the common mushroom and all Agarics and Polyporei.

2. *Gasteromycetes* (*gaster*, a belly). Hymenium, or spore-bearing surface, *enclosed* in a more or less spherical case, called the peridium, which ruptures and expels the spores at maturity in the form of dust, as in the puff-balls.

3. *Coniomycetes*, from the Greek κωνίς, meaning dust, the entire fungus having a *dust-like* appearance. Mildew forms a good example of this family.

4. *Hyphomycetes*, from the Greek ύφα, meaning a thread. *Thread-like* fungi, the filaments being more conspicuous than the spore masses, of which group blue-mould affords an illustration.

The Hymenomycetes (1) is again subdivided into

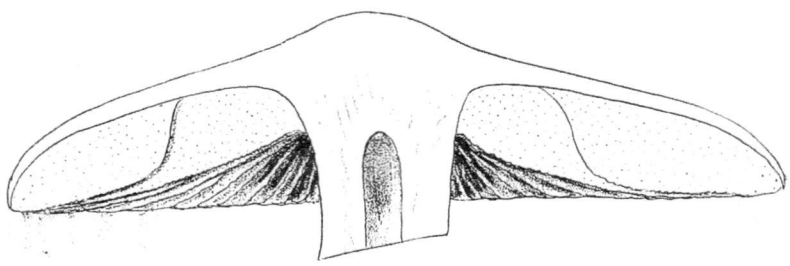

six orders, the discrimination being based on the diverse character of the spore surface. The first of these orders is the *Agaricini*, or gill-bearing fungi, to which our present chapter will be confined.

AGARICINI

In this order the hymenium, or spore-bearing surface, is inferior, *i.e.*, on the under side of the pileus, and is spread over lamellæ or gills, which radiate from the stem of the fungus, and each of which may be separated into two filmy flat divisions.

On the opposite page is shown an Agaric in vertical section, disclosing a full side view of the gills. A highly magnified view of this gill-surface is indicated herewith, duly indexed, the sporophore being shown in the act of shedding its spores from their points of attachment to the four stigmata at the summit.

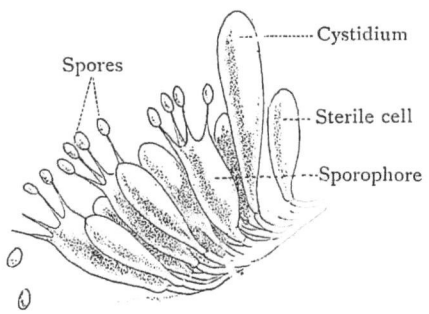

SPORE-SURFACE MAGNIFIED

These fruitful four-pointed sporophores or basidia are intermingled with the cystidia and sterile cells, the whole mass forming the surface of the hymenium. The dissemination of the Agaric is further considered in a later chapter on "Spore-prints."

The most perfect botanical type of the Agarics is the Amanita, already sufficiently dwelt upon.

We will now proceed to the consideration of other examples in which the symbol of the fatal cup is happily absent, and whose identities as esculent species are clearly denoted by individual characteristics.

EDIBLE AGARICS

MEADOW MUSHROOM
Agaricus campestris

Perhaps the one species which enjoys the widest range of popular confidence as the "mushroom" in the lay mind, as distinguished from "toadstool," is the *Agaricus campestris*, known as the "meadow mushroom" (Plate 5). It is the species commonly exposed in our markets. Its cultivation is an important industry, but it often yields an enormous spontaneous harvest in its native haunts. The plate shows a cluster of the mushrooms in their various stages of development, the detached specimen below representing the semi-opened condition in which the fungus is usually gathered for market. It will be observed that the base of the stem is *entirely free from any suggestion of a volva or cup*. As its popular name implies, this species in its wild state is one of the voluntary tributes of our late summer and autumn meadows and pastures, though it may occasionally frequent lawns, shrubberies, and barn-yards. In size it varies from two to three and a half inches across the pileus or cap, which is either smooth or slightly rough, scaly, or scurfy, and creamy white or tawny in color, according to age or variety. The most important distinguishing feature of this species is the color of the gills. If we break away the "veil" in the

"The" mushroom

Description of Campestris

Agaricus campestris

PLATE V

"THE MUSHROOM"

Agaricus campestris

Pileus: At first globular, its edge connected to stem by the veil; then round convex, at length becoming possibly almost flat. Surface dry, downy, or even quite scaly, varying in color from creamy white to light brown. Diameter at full expansion, about three inches.

Gills: Unequal in length; pink when first revealed, becoming brownish, brown, purplish, and finally almost black.

Stem: Solid; of the color of the cap; paler and white in section, retaining the remnant of the veil in a permanent ragged ring.

Spores: Brown.

Taste: Sweet and inviting, and odor agreeable.

Habitat: Pastures, lawns, and open rich soil generally.

Season: Late summer and early autumn, occasionally in spring.

PLATE V

AGARICUS CAMPESTRIS.

unopened specimen, we find them to be of a pallid flesh tint. In the more advanced state they become decidedly pinkish, with age and expansion gradually deepening to purplish, purple-brown, and finally brownish black. The gills are of unequal lengths, as shown in the section. The stem is creamy white and of solid substance, and always shows the remains of the veil in a persistent frill or ring just beneath the cap.

Doubtless a sufficient and satisfactory reason for the universal dignity which this species has acquired as "the mushroom" may be found in **Cultivation of mushrooms** the fact that it is the only species prominently under cultivation, and almost the only one which is sure to respond to the artificial cultivation of its spawn in the so-called "mushroom bed." The "spawn" of the Campestris has thus become a mercantile commodity, duly advertised in the seedsmen's catalogues.

This so-called spawn is in truth nothing but the mycelium, or subterranean vine of the mushroom (see Plate 2), taken from the beds in which **Mushroom "spawn" bed** the mushrooms have been grown, or in which the mycelium has been cultivated. The cultivator simply prepares a "bed" to receive it—duplicating as far as possible the soil conditions from which it was taken, whether from foreign cultivation or his old manure-bed or stable-yard—a rich, warm compost of loam and horse-manure, this latter ingredient being a most important consideration, as the fungus in its several varieties, notably the larger, *Agaricus arvensis*, known as the "horse-mushroom," has followed the track of the horse around the world. These natural conditions having been even approximately fulfilled, will, within two months, generally reward the cultivator with a crop of mushrooms, which, with the continued ramifications of the mycelium permeating the muck as the yeast fungus permeates the home-made loaf, will insure a continual succession of crops for weeks or months, to be renewed spontaneously, perhaps, the following season.

The present volume, having specific reference to fungi in their wild state, and the celebration of their esculent virtues, being thus essentially in antithesis to artificial culture, further consideration of the cultivation of the mushroom is omitted. The reader is referred to the volumes in my bibliographical list, Nos. 8 and 22, in which full instructions will be found.

The Campestris is conspicuous among mushrooms in its ready accommodation to artificial imitation of its native environment. There is no other mushroom which is thus confidently to be relied on. Other species— not a dozen, however, out of the thousands — will occasionally reward the cultivator, who has devoted the most scrupulous care to the humoring of their fastidious conditions of growth. Thus the *Agaricus candicans* of the Italian markets is said to have been successfully raised from chips of the white poplar which have been properly covered with manure. Other species, it is claimed, can be humored from a block of the cob-nut tree after singeing its surface over burned straw, while Dr. Thore claims that both *Boletus edulis*, and *Agaricus pro-*

<small>Species opposed to cultivation</small>

<small>Certain exceptions</small>

cerus are "constantly raised by the inhabitants of his district from a watery infusion of said plants poured upon the ground." The truth of these statements has been denied by authorities, and individual experiment will only tend to discredit their trustworthiness. In general the mushroom or toadstool absolutely refuses to be "coaxed or cajoled." The mycelium of all is practically identical; but species such as the Coprinus, for instance, which are perhaps found growing naturally in company with the Campestris, and whose spawn is similarly transplanted to the artificial environment, will show no sign of reappearance, while its fellow may literally crowd the bed.

The "fairy-ring" mushroom grows year after year upon our lawn, because its mycelium is continually present, simply threading its way outwardly, inch by inch, in the congenial surrounding soil. Instances are reported of the occasional successful establishment of this mushroom in new quarters by the transfer of a clod of earth threaded with mycelium taken from the "fairy-ring" to another lawn, in which the immediate soil conditions happened to be harmonious, and this method of actual transference of the spawn might occasionally be effectual. But the writer, in his limited number of experiments, has never yet been able to propagate a mushroom by a transfer of the *spores* to soil where the conditions would appear to be exactly suitable. On a certain lawn, for instance, every year I obtain a number of the *Coprinus comatus* (Plate 16). Upon another lawn, apparently exactly similar as to soil conditions, I transfer the melting mushroom

<small>Not to be humored</small>

where it sheds its inky spore-solution upon the earth, and yet, after years of waiting, there is no response. Even an absolute transfer of the webby spawn from the original haunt has proven equally without result. Thus while the habitual fungus-hunter comes to recognize a certain logical association between a given character of natural haunt and some certain species of fungi—a prophetic suspicion often immediately fulfilled—as when he inwardly remarks, as he comes upon an open, clear spot in the woods, "This is an ideal haunt for the green Russula," and instantly stumbles upon his specimen; yet he may take the pallid spawn, with a small clod of earth from its roots, and place it in the mould not ten feet distant, apparently in identically auspicious conditions, and it absolutely refuses to be humored. He may mark the spot, and look in vain in its precincts for a decade for his Russula, though the ground in the vicinity be dotted with them.

Year after year I have thrown my refuse specimens of hundreds of species of fungi out of my studio window, over the piazza rail or upon my lawn, yet never with the slightest sign that one of the millions of spores in the species thus sown has vegetated.

Dormant spores

Considering the ready accommodation of the Campestris, the contrast of the fastidiousness in other species is a notable phenomenon. As a rule, "they will not colonize; they will not emigrate; they will not be cheated out of their natural possessions: they refuse to be educated, and stand themselves upon their single leg, as the most independent and contrary growth with which man has to deal."

PLATE VI.—VARIATIONS IN AGARICUS CAMPESTRIS

The Campestris is probably the most protean of all mushrooms, and mycologists are even yet at odds as to the proper botanical disposition of many of the contrasting varieties which it assumes. A few of these are indicated in Plate 6. Indeed, some of these, as in the *Agaricus arvensis*, following, have until quite recently figured as distinct species. In its extreme form it might well so do, but when science is confronted with an intermediate specimen bearing equal affinities to the Campestris and Arvensis — and perhaps reinforced by other individuals which actually merge completely into the Campestris—the discrimination of the Arvensis as a distinct species becomes impossible, and would hardly seem warrantable.

Varieties of the Campestris

Berkeley gives the following selection of the more distinct varieties, not including the Arvensis with *its* variations, and which he considers a distinct species:

1. The so-called "garden mushroom," with its brownish, hairy, scaly cap.
2. *A. pratensis*, in which the pileus is more or less covered with reddish scales, and the flesh as well as gills a pinkish tinge.
3. *A. villaticus*, large size and very scaly.
4. *A. silvicola*, pileus smooth and shining, stem elongated and conspicuously swollen at base; often found in woods.
5. *A. vaporarius*, brown pilose coat which covers the stem as well as the cap, and leaves streaky fragments on the stalk as it elongates.
6. He also figures another marked form, with the cap of a reddish color, completely covered with a pilose coat; the gills being perfectly white in young specimens, and the flesh turning bright red when bruised.

Any one of the above, he admits, are as much entitled to classification as "distinct species" as the Arvensis.

The application of the title "horse-mushroom" to this last-mentioned species was generally supposed to be referable to the same popular tra-

The "horse" mushroom ditions of which we see the analogies in the names horse-weed, horse-nettle, horse-balm, horseradish among the herbs—the prefix "horse" referring to the element of coarseness or rank growth. But in the instance of the mushroom it bears a deeper significance, as this ample cosmopolitan variety of the Campestris, which follows the horse all over the world, from stable and through lane to pasture, and which can only be grown in the manure of this animal, is now generally believed to be a secondary, exaggerated form consequent upon the following conditions:

The spores of the Campestris are shed in myriads in the pastures. The grazing horse no doubt swallows thousands of them, which, upon their return to the soil under especially favorable conditions for growth, vegetate into mycelium, and at length fructify in the full-formed mushroom. The dense white spawn of this species may often be seen beneath the manure in pastures where no sign of the mushroom itself is yet apparent.

During the writing of the present pages I have received from Arizona a letter accompanied with a sketch of a most astonishing mushroom,

A huge variety which my correspondent finds plentifully prevalent in his vicinity, growing in arid sand, even in an exceptionally dry season. He claims that "it is deliciously edible," and he has partaken of it several times. His sketch and description call to mind no existing form of mushroom known to me, though from one peculiarity in particular — namely, its frequently enormous size, "occasionally ten inches in diameter" — one would naturally expect to find it at least notorious, if not famous.

It is plainly an Agaric related to the Campestris, and from the fact of its having "pink gills darker in older specimens" I suspect it to be simply another local masquerade of this same Campestris, which suspicion, by the receipt of further data, I hope soon to verify.

HORSE-MUSHROOM
Agaricus arvensis

This other and larger variety, so readily confounded with the Campestris, demands further and more detailed description. It may frequently be found growing in company with the former, and so closely do the two kinds merge in specimens of equal size that it is often a puzzle to separate the species. Indeed, as already mentioned by some mycologists, the larger form is considered merely as a variety of the Campestris. The accompanying plate (5) may well serve as a portrait of this species also. It frequents the same localities as the former, and is occasionally seen crowded in clusters of crescent **Description** shape, or in scattered rings, while its **of Arvensis** size is generally conspicuous, the solid cream-colored or white cap often expanding to the diameter of seven inches. Its substance discolors to yellowish brown on being bruised.

The stem is less solid than in Campestris, often with a pithlike or even hollow heart. The gills are of unequal length, as in the former species, though of much the same tints of pink and brown and black, though more dingy in the lighter shades. The veil is often more conspicuous, and occasionally appears to be double, the outer or lower more or less ragged or split into a fringe at the edge. The species can hardly be mistaken for any poisonous variety, and, once recognized, its generous size, frequent profusion, and savory qualities make it a tempting quest to the epicure, being considered by many as superior in flavor to its rival, the smaller Campestris.

But this question of gastronomic prestige will perhaps never be finally settled. *De gustibus non est disputandum.* Species considered here by many as the *ne plus ultra* of delicacies, like the Campestris, are discriminated against in other countries, and in Rome, it is said, are even thrown into the Tiber by inspectors and guardians of the public health who find it exposed for sale in the markets. There are those connoisseurs in delicate feasting who consider no other species comparable to this. These fastidious gourmands are in turn viewed with pitying consideration by other superior epicurean feeders with finer sensuous discrimination, who know perfectly well that our woods afford a number of common species which easily consign the Campestris to the fourth or fifth choice as a competitor at the feast.

<small>In matters of taste</small>

The arts of the chef have been exhausted in the savory preparation of this, the most famous of the mushrooms. A few of his ingenious methods are given in a later chapter. Meanwhile most of us will be perfectly contented with our simple " mushrooms on toast."

While the Campestris is generally considered as "the" mushroom, there is another species which almost equally shares the honors in popular favor.

I have alluded to the habit of the horse-mushroom as "growing in crescents or rings." This singular tendency is, however, much more fully exemplified in another fungus, which has thus won the popular patronymic of the "Fairy-ring" Champignon, and which is considered on page 101.

ST. GEORGE'S MUSHROOM
Agaricus gambosus

Another very common example of mushroom in its season of early spring is the *Agaricus gambosus*, or St. George's mushroom, as it is popularly styled in Great Britain, from its usual appearance about the time of St. George's Day, April 23d. In addition to its unusually early season, which is the same with us, and which at this date would be a valuable hint in its identification, it has also the singular habit of growing in rings or clustered in crescents, after the manner of the Fairy-ring Champignon of our lawns.

Remarkably strong odor Add to this, also, a very strong odor, and we have at least three suggestive characteristics to aid us. This odor, according to Dr. Cooke, is so strong as to occasionally become oppressive and overpowering where the fungus is plentiful. Workmen employed to root them out are said to have been so overcome by the odor as to be compelled to desist. Other features of this fungus are noted in Plate 7. The cap varies in size in different individuals, but is occasionally very large—five inches or more in diameter, the average expanse, perhaps, being about three inches. The cap is smooth, thick, and fleshy, suggesting soft kid leather, at first rounded convex, ultimately expanding quite horizontally, and is commonly fissured here and there with irregular cracks, both in its expanse and at its edges. Its color is white, or yellowish white. In surface appearance Dr. Berkeley compared it to a "cracknel biscuit." The gills are yellowish white, very moist and densely crowded, and of various lengths, as indicated in my sectional drawing on the plate, and are, moreover, annexed to the solid stout stem by a toothed border, also shown herewith.

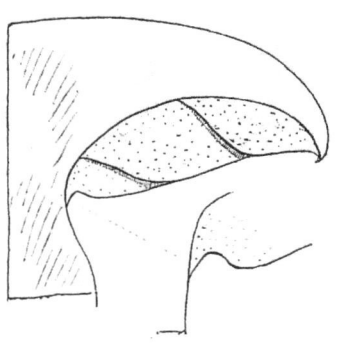

TOOTHED GILLS

The season of this mushroom extends into June, and in its favorite haunt it may occasionally be gathered by the bushel. Opinions are at variance as to the comparative esculent qualities of this species. Certainly delicacy cannot be claimed for it; but those epicures who desire the characteristic *fungus flavor* at its maximum will find it in the Gambosus.

Epicurean opinions

Agaricus gambosus

PLATE VII

ST. GEORGE'S MUSHROOM

Agaricus gambosus

Pileus: Three to six inches in diameter, occasionally much larger; rounded convex, at length more flat and commonly cracked here and there; surface smooth, thick, and fleshy, suggesting soft kid leather. Color, pale ochre or yellowish white.

Gills: Densely crowded; yellowish white; very moist; various lengths; each annexed to stem by a small sharp downward curve.

Stem: Solid; stout; substance creamy white.

Spores: White.

Taste: Highly flavored; by some considered "too gamy."

Odor: Powerfully strong, perhaps rank.

Habitat: Fields, lawns, and pastures, frequently growing in broken rings or crescents.

PLATE VII

AGARICUS GAMBOSUS.

By many fungus-feasters this species is prized as the *ne plus ultra*, and most various are the methods of its culinary preparation, either in the form of mince and fricassee with various meats, suitably seasoned with salt, pepper, and butter, or simply broiled and served on buttered toast. An appetizing recipe for this especial mushroom is given on page 313.

TRUE FAIRY-RING CHAMPIGNON
Marasmius oreades

I remember, as a boy, summer after summer observing upon a certain spot upon our lawn this dense, and at length scattering, ring of tiny yellowish mushrooms, and the aroma, as they simmered on the kitchen stove, is an appetizing memory.

Fairy=ring mushrooms true and false

This species is very common, and inasmuch as it is likely to be confounded with two noxious varieties, it is advisable to bring in prominent contrast the characters of the true and the false.

The true Fairy-ring Champignon is pictured in Plate 8. It is common on lawns and close-cropped pastures, where it is usually seen growing in rings more or less broken, and often several feet in diameter, or in disconnected arcs, the vegetation extending outward year by year. This mushroom is held in great esteem, and frequently grows in such profusion that bushels may be gathered in a small area.

The pileus is buff or cream colored, from one to two inches in diameter, leathery and shrivelled when dry, but when moist, after rain or dew, becoming brownish, soft, and pliable, the conditions perhaps alternating for several days; the skin refuses to be peeled, and in the older, fully opened specimens the centre of the cap is raised in a distinct tiny *mound;* gills, *widely separated,* about ten or twelve to the inch at circumference in average specimens, same color as cap, or paler, unequal in length, curving upward on reaching stem, thus "*free*" from apparent contact with it; stem, equal diameter, tough, fibrous, and tenacious, paler than gills, smooth to the base (*no spines nor down*); cup, none; spores, white; *taste nutty, somewhat aromatic, appetizing;* habitat usually on lawns or pastures.

<small>"True" fairy=ring</small>

The "ring" was long involved in mystery, being attributed to moles, lightning, witchcraft, etc.; and, clothed with popular superstition, has found its way into many folk-legends, and has figured in the lore of elfs and goblins, to whom, in the absence of scientific knowledge, the strange, fungus-haunted circle was referred, the "ring" being applied not merely to the circle of mushrooms themselves, but especially to the clearly defined ring of clear, fresh grass surrounding the central, more faded area. But the fairies no longer dance their moonlight rigadoon upon the charmed circle of the champignon, nor do the nimble elves "rear their midnight mushrooms" upon the rings of lush grass as of old, for science has stepped in and cleared up the mystery. The Rev. M. J. Berkeley, in his *Outlines to British Fungology,* thus completely rescues the "fairy-ring" from the domain of poetry and reduces it to prosaic fact:

<small>Traditions of the mystic "ring"</small>

Marasmius oreades

PLATE VIII

FAIRY RING CHAMPIGNON

Marasmius oreades

Pileus: Convex at first, becoming flat, with a mound at centre, at juncture of stem; texture, tough and pliable when moist, brittle in drying, alternating between these two conditions with rain and sun ; color, reddish buff at first, becoming cream colored when old, when it is usually quite wrinkled.

Gills: Broad, and quite separated; about ten or twelve to the inch at rim in large specimens; unequal in length; deep cream color; clearing the stem as they curve upward towards cap.

Stem: Solid; equal diameter; tough and fibrous; naked and smooth at base.

Spores: White.

Taste: Sweet, "nutty," and appetizing.

Odor: Aromatic and pleasant.

Habitat: Pastures and lawns, generally growing in rings or curved lines.

Diameter of pileus, full expansion, one to two inches.

PLATE

MARASMIUS OREADES.

"These rings are sometimes of very ancient date, and attain such enormous dimensions as to be distinctly visible on a hill-side for a great distance. It is believed that they originate from a single fungus whose growth renders the soil immediately beneath unfit for its reproduction. The spawn, however, spreads all around, and in the second year produces a crop, whose spawn spreads again, the exhausted soil behind forbidding its return in that direction. Thus the circle is continually increased, and extends indefinitely till some cause intervenes to destroy it. If the spawn does not spread on all sides at first, an arc of a circle only is produced. The manure arising from the dead fungi of former years makes the grass peculiarly vigorous around, so as to render the circle visible even when there is no external appearance of fungus, and the contrast is often stronger from that behind being killed by the old spawn. This mode of growth is far more common than is supposed, and may be observed constantly in our woods, where the spawn can spread only in the soil or among the leaves and decaying fragments which cover it."

[margin: The "ring" explained]

Many recipes are recommended for the preparation of this mushroom, some of which are given in a later chapter, including the method of desiccation so commonly employed with other species, and by which the champignon may be kept for ready use throughout the winter months.

[margin: Various recipes]

In its fresh state, according to J. M. Berkeley, "When

of good size and quickly grown, it is perhaps the best of all fungi for the table, whether carefully fried or stewed with an admixture of finely mixed herbs and a minute portion of garlic. It is at the same time tender and easy of digestion, and when once its use is known and its character ascertained, no species may be eaten with less fear. It is so common in some districts that bushels may be gathered in a day."

FALSE OR POISON CHAMPIGNON
Marasmius urens

There are two other species of mushroom which might possibly be mistaken for the above by the casual eye, but which are easily distinguishable on careful examination. The first of these is the false Champignon (Plate 9, fig. 1). The most important distinguishing features are italicized. They will be seen to afford a striking contrast to the true edible species in these especial characters.

The pileus is pale buff, convex, central mound absent; the cap varies from one-half to one and a half inches in diameter, and is thus slightly smaller than the "true" fairy-ring; gills, yellowish brown, narrow, and *crowded*, twenty-five or more to the inch at circumference in good specimen, curving upward at junction with stem, thus "free" from actual attachment; stem, solid, clothed with *whitish down*, especially noticeable at the base; cup, none; *taste, acrid*. This last quality alone should distinguish the species, which, moreover, usually grows in *woods*, though occasionally found upon the lawn in association with the edible species.

Marasmius urens
Marasmius peronatus

PLATE IX

POISONOUS CHAMPIGNONS

Marasmius urens

Pileus: Pale buff in color; tough and fleshy; flat convex, becoming depressed and at length wrinkled; one to two inches in diameter.

Gills: Unequal, cream colored, becoming brownish; much closer together than in the true Champignon, hardly reaching the stem proper.

Stem: Solid; fibrous; pale, its surface more or less covered with white, flocculent down, and densely clothed with white down at base.

Taste: Acrid.

Habitat: Lawns and pastures, often in association with the edible *M. oreades*.

Marasmius peronatus

Pileus: Reddish buff; convex slightly flattened at top, becoming convex by expansion; very wrinkled when old; diameter, at full expansion, between one and two inches.

Gills: Thin and crowded; creamy, becoming light reddish brown, continuing slightly down stem by a short, abrupt curve.

Stem: Solid; fibrous; pale, densely clothed with stiff yellow hairs at base.

Taste: Acrid.

Habitat: In woods, among dead leaves, etc.

PLATE IX

POISONOUS CHAMPIGNONS.

MARASMIUS URENS.   M. PERONATUS

POISONOUS FAIRY-RING MUSHROOM
Marasmius peronatus

The other false species (Plate 9, fig. 2) still more closely simulates the "fairy-ring," but may be identified by the growth of *spines* at the base of the stalk. The gills are also *annexed to the stalk* by a small, sharp, *recurved tooth*. Like the previous spurious species, it is found in *woods*, and is rarely to be seen in association with the true Champignon or in its peculiar haunt.

THE PASTURE MUSHROOM
Agaricus (Lepiota) procerus

One of the most readily recognized of our wild mushrooms is the pasture or parasol Agaric (*Agaricus procerus*), a cluster of which in various stages of development is shown in Plate 10. It is frequently abundant in pasture-lands, and is occasionally found in woods. Its conspicuous cap sometimes measures six inches or more in diameter, the centre being abruptly raised in a mound. The pileus is at first egg-shaped. The color of the full specimen is pale-brown or buff, more or less spotted with darker brown shaggy patches, generally arranged in somewhat concentric order. The skin of the cap is thick and somewhat tough, especially in drying. The gills are almost pure white in early specimens, slightly creamy later, and unequal in length. Stem, often six or eight inches high, proportionately slender, and of equal diameter, bulbous at base, but without a cup, hollow, fibrous, finely speckled or streaked with brown, and deeply inserted in the cap, at which juncture, by a narrow flat space, as shown in the section drawing below, it is *distinctly free* from contact with the gills. The remnants of the veil are in the form of a more or less detachable ring encircling

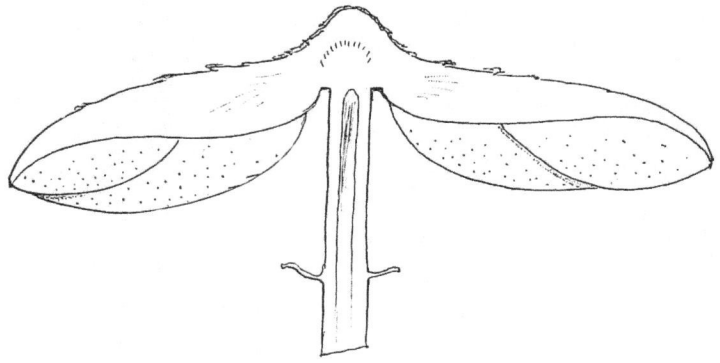

the stem. The spores are white and odorous. The flavor, when raw, is distinctly nutty, aromatic, sweet, and palatable; when dry, slightly pungent.

This species is cosmopolitan, and is a great favorite on the Continent—in France being known as the *Coulemelle*, in Italy as *Bubbola maggiore*, and in Spain as *Cogomelos*. It is by many considered as the choicest of all mushrooms, and is indeed a delicious morsel when quickly broiled over coals, seasoned to taste with salt and pepper and butter melted in the gills, and served hot on buttered toast. Other recipes are noted in a later chapter. The scurfy spots and stems should be removed before cooking.

Simple recipe

Agaricus procerus

PLATE X

THE PASTURE MUSHROOM

Agaricus procerus

Pileus: At first egg-shaped, finally expanded like a parasol four to seven inches in diameter, the apex raised in a prominent mound or "umbo." Color pale buff or creamy, occasionally almost pure white, more or less regularly spotted with the brown shaggy patches of the separating epidermis, which remains of the pale brown color on the "umbo." Skin thick and somewhat tough; substance hygrometric, drying and swelling naturally in its haunts.

Gills: Unequal in length; crowded; at first almost white, finally becoming creamy or pale buff.

Stem: Tall, slender, equal, hollow, and fibrous; bulbous at base, but with no sign of a "cup;" separated from the gills above by a distinct space; surface streaked and speckled with brown, encircled by a loose ring.

Spores: White, and, like the whole plant, fragrant aromatic—more so, perhaps, than any other fungus.

Taste: Distinctly sweet and "nutty," slightly pungent when dry.

Habitat: Pastures and fields, occasionally woods.

Season: Summer.

Agaricus Procerus

This species is especially free from the swarming grubs too commonly found in mushrooms. It is high-

Hygrometric properties

ly hygrometric, dries naturally even while standing in the pasture, in which condition it is decidedly aromatic in fragrance and nutty sweet to the taste, as described. Indeed, it is sometimes called "the nut mushroom." Absorbing moisture from the dews and rains, it again becomes pulpy and enlarged, thus alternating for days between its juicy and dry condition, in which latter state it may be gathered and kept for winter use. It is a palatable morsel at all times, but especially in the prime of its first expansion, each successive alternation, with its gradual loss of spores, affecting its full flavor.

THE RUSSULA GROUP

Among the wild species of mushrooms which the novice might possibly mistake for the common "mushroom" of the markets—which is popularly supposed to be the *only edible* variety, as distinguished from "toadstools"—is the Russula group. They are extremely frequent in our woods from spring to late autumn, and have many features in common. Their caps vary in color from a gray-green, suggesting cheese-mould, to olive-red, scarlet-red,

Generic characters

and purplish. The gills are generally of the same length, or practically so, occasionally double-branched, beginning at the stem and usually extending to the rim of the cap, at which portion they are covered by the mere skin of the pileus, a slightly fluted appearance being observable from above, which indicates the location of the radiating laminæ below (Plate 12, fig. 6).

The stem may be white or cream-colored, or perhaps stained or mottled with the color of the cap.

There are at least four of these edible Russulæ that we are certain of meeting in our walks in the woods: The green Russula (*R. virescens*), with its mottled cap of mouldy or sage green; the various-gilled Russula (*R. heterophylla*), varying in the lengths of its gill plates; the purple Russula (*R. lepida*), whose cap varies from bright red to dull purple; and the red Russula (*R. alutacea*), which presents a variety of shades of red, from bright to dull. Having once identified the Russula as a group, or the common characteristics of the genus, we may take our pick from all of these delicious species for the table; but we must avoid one other member of the genus, also quite common, and which frequently masquerades in the guise of some of the bright red varieties above mentioned. This is the *R. emetica*, whose obnoxious qualities are indicated by its classical surname, and which will be separately considered.

Principal species

THE GREEN RUSSULA
Agaricus (Russula) virescens

Our first species, the green Russula, is to be found throughout the summer in hard-wood groves, and is apt to frequent the same immediate locality from year to year. I know one such veritable mushroom bed in the woods near by, where I am almost certain of my mess of Russulæ almost any day in their season. This species is shown in its various stages of development and also in section in Plate 11. Its substance is *firm* and solid *creamy white*. The pileus, at first almost hemispherical, as it pushes its way through the earth, at length becomes convex, with a slight hollow at the centre, and later ascends in a gentle slope from centre to rim. Its color is sage green, or mouldy green, usually quite unbroken in tint at centre, but more or less disconnected into spots as it ap-

Specific characters

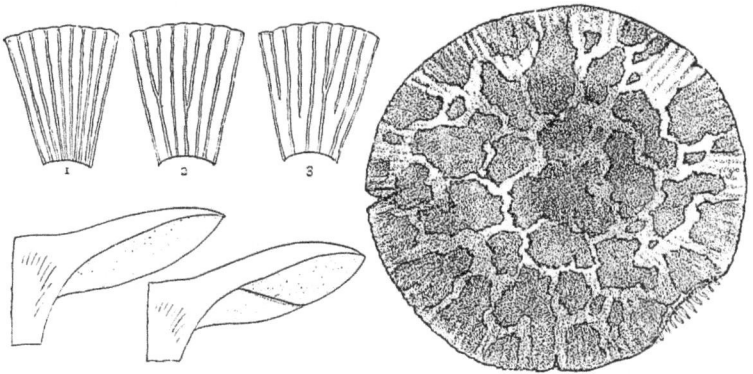

RUSSULA VIRESCENS
(Showing mottled cap of occasional specimen, and variations in gills. 1 *even;* 2 *forked;* 3 *dimidiate.*)

proaches the circumference by the gradual expansion of the cap, the creamy undertint appearing like network between the separated patches of color. The substance of the cap becomes gradually thinned towards the circumference, where the mere cuticle connects the gills, the position of these gills being observable from above in a faint fluting of the edge, a peculiarity of all the Russulæ. The cuticle peels readily some distance from the edge, leaving the projecting tips of the gills exposed in a row of comb-like teeth, but usually adheres towards the centre of cap. The gills, with rare exceptions, are *all of the same length*, white or creamy in color, firm and thick, but *very brittle*, easily broken into fragments by a rude touch, a characteristic of all the group; spores, white. The stem is short, stout, and solid, and usually tapers towards the base. There is no vestige of a cup or veil at *any* stage of growth.

A fine specimen of the green Russula should measure five inches in diameter when fully open, but three inches is probably the average size.

When once acquainted with the above as a *type* of the Russula group, noting the firm substance, straight, equal gills, and their brittle texture; the sweet, nutty flavor common to all the edible species, these become readily identified, the *noxious* Russulæ, as in the brilliant pink or scarlet *R. emetica* (Plate 13), being *acrid* and *peppery* to the taste.

The noxious Russulæ

In an auspicious season and in a congenial habitat —usually an open wood with scant undergrowth and preferably raked clean of dead leaves—the green Russula is often abundant. Familiarity even with this one species will often afford a sufficiency of fungus food during its season. A lady amateur mycophagist of the writer's acquaintance, whose home is located at the border of such a wood as is above described, and who is especially fond of the green Russula, is never at a loss for this especially prized tidbit as a

Green Russula often sufficient

Russula virescens

PLATE XI

THE GREEN RUSSULA

Russula virescens

Pileus: Very firm; solid, dull, dry-surfaced, as with a fine "flock"; mouldy green or creamy, with sage-greenish broken spots more united at centre; occasionally entirely green, with warty patches of darker hue. At first globular, then convex with flat top, at length expanded and hollowed towards centre.

Gills: Pale, creamy white; commonly all of equal length, but frequently unequal and forked; very brittle, breaking in pieces at a rude touch.

Stem: Solid; creamy white; no veil.

Taste: Very mild, sweet, and nut-like.

Habitat: In woods—July–September.

Diameter of pileus, ideal specimen, four inches.

PLATE XI

RUSSULA VIRESCENS.

reward for her daily stroll among the trees. A visitor may often see upon her buffet a small glass dish filled with the mushrooms, nicely scraped and cut in pieces — an ever-present relish between meals. For even in their natural state, as she discriminatingly says, they are "as sweet as chestnuts." This is especially the case with the "buttons" or younger specimens.

PURPLE RUSSULA
Russula lepida

This, perhaps the most common species, is figured in Plate 12, fig. 3. It corresponds with the foregoing in size as well as in general shape, firm text-

RUSSULA LEPIDA — CONTORTED AND CRACKED PILEUS

ure, and friable nature of the gills. The pileus of this species frequently assumes eccentric shapes, or is often cracked, as seen in the accompanying cut. Its name of "purple" is probably local in its application, as it is known also as the *red* Russula, neither of which titles is at all distinctive. Indeed, the color of the *cap* is often a misleading character for identification, as a given species may vary greatly in this particular. This feature is thus generally omitted in purely scientific descriptions, more dependence being placed upon the tint of the flesh and that of the spore surface, the laminæ or gills, which are more permanent and reliable as a character. Thus, in the present species, *R. lepida*, the tint of the pileus or cap is often of a deep dull purplish red or ruddy wine color. Another authority describes it as violet-red and cherry-red or slightly tawny, paler at circumference. Berkeley, in his *British Fungi*, omits any reference to the color of the cap, as evidently of little value in identification. But from numerous examples gathered by the present writer, the color may, I think, be safely averaged under the general hue of dark, subdued red inclining to maroon. The surface is dull, as with a fine dust or plum-like bloom, and thus without polish. Occasional specimens appear almost velvety in the sheen of surface. But the tints of the flesh and the gills are always uniform, the *leaflets* or gills being *pure white* or very slightly creamy, continuous from stem to rim or occasionally forked, not crowded, curved in outline in open specimen, with broadest width near the circumference of cap. The flesh is white or slightly creamy, firm and compact as in the former species, with the same variations of outline

Color of cap misleading

Specific characters

Edible Russulæ

EDIBLE RUSSULÆ

1. Russula heterophylla—Variable Russula

Pileus: Firm, solid; greenish or pinkish-gray; at first convex, with flat top, ultimately rising from centre to rim.
Gills: Milk-white; extremely brittle, like all the Russulæ, and easily crumbled (see Fig. 7); long, short, and forked intermixed. Fig. 5.
Stem: Milk-white; solid.
Taste: Mild and sweet.

2. Russula alutacea—Yellow-gilled Russula

Pileus: Firm, solid; shape as in above; color very variable, from bright to deep red; cuticle thin at rim, where the lines of junction of gills are readily discernible from above by the depressed channels. Fig. 6.
Gills: Equal, brittle, broad; yellow-buff color in all stages. Fig. 4.
Stem: Solid; milk-white, commonly stained or streaked with red towards the base.
Taste: Sweet and nut-like.

3. Russula lepida—Purple Russula

Pileus: In shape like above, varying in color from bright red to dull, subdued purplish, with a distinct bloom.
Gills: White, broad, principally even, occasionally forked as in Fig. 1; like the above, extremely brittle. Fig. 7.
Stem: Solid; white, usually stained and streaked with pink. Fig. 8.
Taste: Sweet, and similar to above.

Average diameter of extended pileus of each of these species about three and one-half inches; veil absent in each.
Habitat: All grow in woods—July–September.

Edible Russulae.
RUSSULA HETEROPHYLLA   R. ALUTACEA   R. LEPIDA

from early stage to maturity. The stem is white, solid, and generally more or less tinted or streaked vertically with rose or pale crimson (Fig. 8). The taste of the flesh is sweet and appetizing.

YELLOW-GILLED RUSSULA
Russula alutacea

Our third example of the Russula is one which is also quite common in our woods, and which might in the extreme variation of its color be confounded with the last by a careless observer, as indeed both might be still further confounded with the poisonous member bearing the red tint, and which will be hereafter considered. The *Russula alutacea* (Pl. 12, figs. 2, 4, 6) is a delicious species. In general size and contour it resembles the foregoing. The color of the cap varies from bright-red to blood-red or even approaching the purplish red of the preceding species, lightening towards edge. But we have a clear distinction in the color of the *gills*, which are *distinctly yellowish*, pale ochre, or nankeen, in all stages of the mushroom, *or even tawny* in old specimens. They are, moreover, usually *all of even length*, being straight and continuous from stem to circumference of pileus, none of them forked, their juncture with the edge of the cap being clearly manifest from above by the thinness of the cuticle. The flesh is white, stem firm and solid, white and smooth, often tinted with pink or red. The flesh of the cap often appears pinkish upon peeling the cuticle from the edge. The taste resembles that of the previous species—sweet and nutty.

[margin: Botanical characters]

VARIOUS-GILLED RUSSULA
Russula heterophylla

Growing in company with both of the above is frequently to be seen another species, which is somewhat protean in its accomplishments of color, but which in the character of its gills, as implied in its scientific name, gives us a ready means of identification—*heterophylla*—various-leaved (Pl. 12, figs. 1 and 5). In the previous examples of Russulæ the gills have been commonly straight, continuous from stem to edge of cap, or more rarely forked and continuous in the bifurcation. In the present species we have both of these conditions, combined also with what are called *dimidiate* gills, or *shorter* leaflets, which reach, perhaps, only half-way from rim to stem, all crowded together and alternating. The color of the cap is very variable—occasionally pinkish-ash color or dull pinkish-gray inclining to green or olive or even red. Its surface is smoother than in the foregoing species, being almost polished, and the pellicle of the cap is usually noticeably thinner. Having found such a specimen, possessing also all the other attributes of shape, firmness of flesh, and dry brittleness of gills, if tasted and found sweet in flavor it may be eaten without the slightest fear, and like its congeners will be found a delicious morsel, whether nibbled raw, as the squirrels are so fond of doing, or served hot on toast as an entrée, or otherwise prepared according to taste.

Botanical characters

Various methods prevail in the culinary preparation of the Russula mushroom, many of which are suggested among the receipts in another chapter, but broiling is perhaps the most simple and generally satisfactory. Having thoroughly cleaned the top, or, if desired, peeled the cuticle, place the mushrooms on a gridiron over a hot fire, gills downward, for a few moments, sufficient to allow them to be heated through without scorching. Then reverse them and repeat the process, melting a small piece of butter in the gills and salting and peppering to taste; serve hot on toast or in the platter with roast beef or fowl. They are also delicious fried in the ordinary way, either with or without batter.

Delicious broiled Russula

The Russula is particularly in favor among the fungus-eating insects, whose rapid development and

AN INFESTED SPECIMEN

voracity are consistently related to the ephemeral nature of their food. A Russula specimen showing barely a trace of insect life when gathered will sometimes prove literally honey-combed and totally unfit for food in the space of twenty-four hours. It is therefore well to cut each specimen in sections before venturing upon its preparation for the table, and to profit thereby according to our individual fastidiousness, as suggested on page 37.

While the above esculent species of Russulæ are being familiarized by the tyro, he must now be put on guard against a certain dangerous species of the group, which is sure to claim his attention, being especially fond of the good company of its cousins, and likely to do some mischief through its frequent disguise.

POISONOUS OR EMETIC MUSHROOM
Russula emetica

The variability in the coloring of the three edible species already described brings them occasionally into such close similarity with the gamut of color of the one common poisonous species of the group that this enemy must also be familiarized ere we venture too confidently upon our Russula diet. The *Russula emetica* (Plate 13), as its name implies, is at war with luxurious gastronomy, but its distinction from the harmless varieties is, after all, quite simple. Its frequent general similarity to *R. lepida* and *R. alutacea* is such that the amateur should hardly rely upon the botanical characters alone. There is but one safe, as it is a simple, rule for him: *He should taste every specimen of his Russula of whatever kind*

<small>The poisonous Russula</small>

Russula emetica

PLATE XIII

POISONOUS OR EMETIC MUSHROOM

Russula emetica

Pileus: Expansion two to four inches; color varying from pale bright pink to deep scarlet; very smooth.

Gills: Broad (in section), mostly equal in length, and continuous from edge of cap to stem; not crowded; white.

Stem: White or pinkish.

Spores: White, like all Russulæ.

Taste: Hot and peppery.

Habitat: Woods, with other Russulæ.

Season: July–September.

NOTE.—While, for conservative reasons, the poisonous reputation of this species is here perpetuated, it is quite probable that such condemnation is unwarranted, except as to the *raw* mushroom. The peppery tang and demoralizing powers are now claimed to be dissipated in cooking, and the *Emetica* will doubtless soon be more generally included with its congeners among the esculents, thus bringing the entire genus *Russula* into the friendly group.

Captain Charles McIlvaine is largely responsible for this conversion in favor of *Emetica*. His individual experiments warrant him in pronouncing this species "as good as the rest" when cooked. Others of the writer's acquaintance, following his example, echo his opinion.

PLATE

RUSSULA EMETICA.
(POISONOUS)

before venturing upon its use as food. All of the sweet and palatable Russulæ are esculent. When he chances upon the *R. emetica* he will be aware of its important demoralizing resources in the peppery-hot tingle of his tongue, which, if not instantly perceived, will within the space of a minute assert itself distinctly. All such acrid specimens should be excluded, as a single one would be sufficient to bring an ignominious denouement to an otherwise delectable feast. In the typical *R. emetica* the pileus is a bright, brilliant red — which, as we have said, is very variable, as indicated in our plate — often polished and shining; the gills broad, *equal, straight, continuous, not crowded,* and *white,* as is the flesh beneath the peeled cuticle. The stem is white or pink. The cap will average, perhaps, three inches in diameter, though occasionally reaching the dimensions indicated by the marks in plate, or even larger.

A warning tang

THE OYSTER MUSHROOM
Agaricus ostreatus

What a mass of nutritious food do we occasionally pass in innocence or spurn with our foot upon the old stump or fallen log in the woods!—a neglected feast, indeed, if the specialists on edible fungi are to be believed; a feast, in truth, for a big family, if we chance upon even an average cluster of the "vegetable oyster," which is pictured in Plate 14.

I have commonly observed this species, the *Agaricus ostreatus*, in the autumn, and this is the season given for its appearance in Europe by the authorities;

but according to certain American specialists, notably Charles McIlvaine, it is common in our woods in spring, even as early as March, and through the summer. It is usually found in large clusters, similar to our illustration, growing upon decaying stumps and the trunks of various trees. The "oyster" is a gilled mushroom which grows *sidewise* from its position, the stem being usually lateral and very short, though occasionally quite prolonged, the two varieties being indicated in the accompanying cut.

A "vegetable oyster"

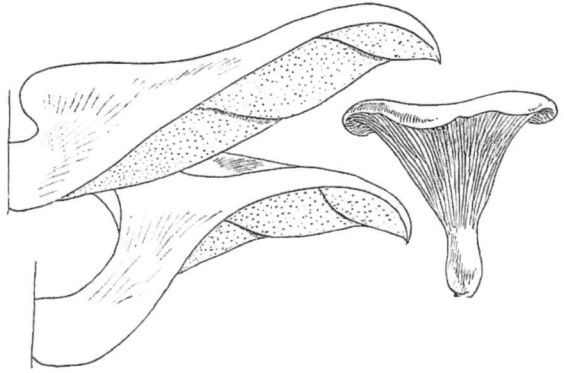

AGARICUS OSTREATUS—Variations in Form

The individual mushroom may be five or six inches in breadth, a cluster affording several pounds in weight. The color of the upper surface is light brown or buff, varying to yellowish-ashen, according to age, and the gills are dirty white of various lengths; spores white.

This species and the one following belong to the subdivision of the typical genus Agaricus, called Leucospori — white spored. The division has many

Agaricus ostreatus

PLATE XIV

THE OYSTER MUSHROOM

Agaricus ostreatus

Pileus: Four to six inches in diameter; smooth. Color, dull, light yellowish, sometimes pale ochre or grayish.

Gills: Dingy white; of various lengths, extending down the stem.

Stem: Short or obsolete; on the side of pileus.

Spores: White.

Taste: Agreeable; suggesting the flavor of the cooked oyster; texture tough in older specimens.

Odor: Pleasant.

Habitat: On old tree trunks and fallen logs, occasionally in dense masses.

PLATE XIV

AGARICUS OSTREATUS.

sub-genera. The particular sub-genus in which these are included is the Pleurotus, or *side-foot* mushrooms, as they are sometimes called.

Another earlier species with which *A. ostreatus* might be confounded (*A. euosmus*) has spores of a rosy pinkish or lilac hue, a sufficient identification, and is accounted injurious.

THIRTY POUNDS OF VEGETABLE MEAT

The clustering growth of the "Oyster Mushroom" frequently attains huge proportions, as will be seen from the above reproduction of a photograph sent to me by a correspondent. The dimensions of the mass are easily judged by the height of the gun leaning against the tree, and introduced for comparison.

This "Oyster Mushroom" should be gathered in its young state, and may be served in various ways. Broiling over the coals, gills upward, seasoning with butter, pepper, and salt during the cooking, is a favorite method with most of the Agarics, but a well-known fungus epicure claims that this mushroom "may be cooked in any way that an oyster is, and will be found fine eating."

<small>Broiled oyster recipe</small>

The average specimen will probably prove more ashen in hue than those represented in my plate.

THE ELM MUSHROOM
Agaricus ulmarius

This edible species of mushroom, allied to the foregoing, and which grows in similar clusters on the elm-tree, is the *Agaricus ulmarius* (Plate 15). While much difference of opinion prevails regarding the appetizing qualities of this mushroom or its right to a place among the esculents, this varying individual judgment has doubtless often had direct reference to the character of the particular specimen chosen for trial. Dr. M. C. Cooke is not disposed to place a high appreciation upon its qualities. "It has been customary," he says, "to regard this and some of its allies [presumably in allusion to the preceding] as alimentary, but there is no doubt that they could all be very well spared from the list." Opposed to this uncomplimentary aspersion is the testimony of other

<small>Appetizing qualities</small>

Agaricus ulmarius

PLATE XV

THE ELM MUSHROOM

Agaricus ulmarius

Pileus: From three to five inches in diameter. Color, pale yellow or buff; smooth in young specimen, fissured, spotted, and leathery at maturity. Flesh in section white.

Gills: Dingy white, becoming tawny at maturity, extending down the stem.

Stem: Various in length, occasionally very short and attached to side of pileus; generally longer as in Plate, and "off centre"; white; substance solid.

Spores: White.

Taste: Suggesting fish when cooked.

Odor: Pleasant.

Habitat: Trunk of elm or from surfaces of broken or sawn branches. Often growing in dense masses covering several square feet.

PLATE XV

AGARICUS ULMARIUS.

authorities who claim that "it is most delectable" and "a delicious morsel." Certain it is that in its young and tender condition only is it fit for food, as it becomes progressively tough in consistency towards maturity.

As its specific name implies—*Ulmus*—this mushroom is devoted to the elm, upon whose trunk and branches it may be often seen, either singly, which is rare, or in great dense masses, sometimes covering a space of several square feet, often, unfortunately, at an inaccessible height from the ground. I have in my possession a photograph which has been sent to me by an interested correspondent representing a dead tree trunk, apparently a foot in diameter, densely covered to a height of seven feet from the ground with a mass of the *A. ulmarius*—and presumably representing thirty or forty pounds in weight. This species is most frequently seen on apparently healthy branches, or growing from the wood of a severed limb. Its season is late summer and autumn.

<small>Massive growth</small>

A small cluster of these mushrooms is seen in Plate 15. They afford a good refutation of the oldtime discriminating "ban," which excluded all mushrooms which grow "sidewise," or "upon wood." The individual mushroom of this species is a horizontal grower, sometimes with a barely noticeable or obsolete stem; in other specimens this portion being quite distinct and an inch or more in length, and firm and solid in texture. The upper surface is pale

<small>Botanical characters</small>

yellow or buff, smooth in the younger specimens, becoming disfigured by spots and fissures with age. The flesh is white, as also are the gills, though more dingy, becoming tawny-tinted with maturity, when the entire mushroom becomes quite leathery in substance, and might well awaken doubts as to its digestibility. The spores are white.

This fungus is known in some sections as the "Fish Mushroom," referring to its peculiar flavor, the appropriateness of which appellation is suggested in the incident related by Mr. Palmer, and quoted in my last chapter.

SHAGGY-MANE MUSHROOM
Coprinus comatus

Upon a certain spot on the lawn of one of my neighbors, year after year, without fail, there springs up a most singular crop. For the first two seasons of its appearance it was looked upon with curious awe by the proprietors of the premises, and usually ignominiously spurned with the foot by the undiscriminating and destructive small boy. One day I observed about five pounds of this fungus delicacy thus scattered piecemeal about the grass, and my protest has since spared the annual crop for my sole benefit. It usually makes its appearance in late September, and continues in intermittent crops until November. A casual observer happening upon a cluster of the young mushrooms might imagine that he beheld a convention of goose eggs standing on end in the grass, their summits spotted with brown.

A plebeian toadstool

Coprinus comatus

PLATE XVI

THE SHAGGY-MANE MUSHROOM

Coprinus comatus

Pileus: Egg-shaped in young specimens; at length more cylindrical, and finally expanded, melting away in inky fluid. Color, creamy white, becoming black at edge with advancing age, as is also the case with the shaggy points upon its surface, which generally cover the pileus.

Gills: Crowded; equal in length; creamy white in young specimens, becoming pink, brown, and finally black, and always moist.

Stem: Cylindrical; creamy white; hollow, or with a loose cottony pith.

Spores: Black, falling away in drops.

Taste: Sweet, which applies only to the pink or white condition, at which time alone the species is considered esculent.

Habitat: Lawns, pastures, gardens, and rich grounds in the neighborhood of barns. etc.; usually grows in dense clusters.

Diameter of cylindrical pileus in average specimens, two inches.

One of the most easily identified of all mushrooms.

PLATE XVI

COPRINUS COMATUS

If one of them is examined, it is seen to be a curious short-stemmed mushroom which never fully expands (Plate 16), perhaps five inches high, and whose surface is curiously decorated with shaggy

A DINNER FOR A FAMILY

patches. In its early stages it is white and singularly egglike, but later becomes brownish, its curved shaggy points finally changing to almost black. The concealed gills are crowded and of equal length, at first creamy white, but gradually changing through a whole gamut of pinks, sepias, and browns until they become black, at which time the whole substance of the cap melts on its elongated stalk—

Inky deliquescence *deliquesces into an unsightly inky paste, which besmears the grass* and ultimately leaves only the bare white stem standing in its midst, a peculiar method of dissemination which distinguishes the group Coprinus, of which it is the most conspicuous example. This is the "shaggy-mane" mushroom, *Coprinus comatus*, the specific name signifying a wig — "from the fancied resemblance to a wig on a barber's block." Even a brief description is unnecessary with its portrait before us. It is a savory morsel, and it cannot be confounded with any other fungus. It frequently grows in such dense, crowded masses that a single group will afford a dinner for a family.

It should be gathered while the gills are in the early white or pink stage, and may be prepared for the table in various ways, either broiled or fried, as described for previous species, or stewed with milk, or otherwise served according to the culinary hints in our later chapter, in which a special recipe for this species is found.

In a recent stroll down the main street of Litchfield, Connecticut, I observed, over the fence in a front door-yard of a summer resident, just such a dense cluster of the shaggy Coprinus, the proprietor of the premises, an appreciative habitué of Delmonico's at other seasons of the year, complacently reading his morning paper in his piazza, little dreaming

Coprinus atramentarius

PLATE XVII

THE INKY TOADSTOOL

Coprinus atramentarius

Pileus: Fleshy, moist; at first egg-shaped; of a Quaker-drab, dirty white, or even pale brownish color; at length becoming expanded, umbrella-like, when it melts away in inky drops.

Gills: Broad and crowded, not adhering to stem at top; creamy white in young species, becoming pinkish gray, and at length black.

Stem: Firm; white; hollow.

Spores: Black; shed in liquid drops.

Taste: Sweet. as is also the odor, which applies to its early stage only.

Habitat: About old decaying stumps and rotten wood, gardens, rich lawns, and barn-yards; usually growing in clusters, often very dense.

Diameter of pileus, young state, two inches.

PLATE XVII

COPRINUS ATRAMENTARIUS.

of the twenty pounds of dainty diet, fit for a king, so easily available.

INKY MUSHROOM
Coprinus atramentarius

In frequent company with the foregoing will be found another allied species, *Coprinus atramentarius* (Plate 17), with the same inky propensities, which is scarcely less delicious as an article of food. In this species the shaggy feature is absent, there being merely a few obscure slightly raised stains at the summit, of a brownish color. The stem is white and hollow. The surface of the pileus is smooth and of a Quaker-drab color, occasionally dirty-white, or with a slight shade of ochre, moist to the touch, darkened by rubbing. In the eatable stage the caps are drooping, as shown in the cluster on the plate, while the mature specimen expands considerably before its inky deliquescence. Its texture when young is firm, and the thick gray cuticle peels readily, leaving an appetizing nutty-flavored morsel, delicious even when raw. The inky Agaric is frequent about barn-yards, gardens, and old stumps in woods, and usually grows in such crowded masses that the central individuals are compressed into hexagonal shape. Like the previous variety, it should be collected for food while its gills are in the white or pink stage.

Cordier claims that all the species of Coprinus are eatable at this stage. The profusion in which they occasionally abound renders it often a simple matter to obtain a bushel of them in a few minutes.

(Botanical characters)

Like the foregoing, a large cluster of these mushrooms leaves a most unsightly spot on the lawn. A diluted solution of this melting substance, as Cooke assures us, has been used "to replenish the ink-bottle. The resemblance is so complete that it may readily be employed as a substitute, all that is required being to boil and strain it, and add a small quantity of corrosive sublimate to prevent its turning mouldy." It may also be employed as pigment. It is, indeed, quite possible to paint the portrait of Coprinus with its own dark sepia, as the author has personally demonstrated. (See head-piece to "Illustrations.")

Coprinus ink

MILKY MUSHROOM
Lactarius deliciosus

Prominent among the fungi which give unmistakable characters for their identification is the genus Lactarius, or milky mushrooms, another group of the agarics or gilled fungi, from which we will select for our first example the *Lactarius deliciosus*, or orange-milk Agaric (Plate 18). The figure will itself almost serve to identify it in its advanced open stage. Having found a specimen resembling our illustration, and anywhere from three to five inches in expanse, its general upper surface *dull reddish-orange* in color, more or less plainly banded with darker red, it is safe to predict that when its surface or gills are broken an exudation of milky juice will follow. If this exudation is orange or *deep yellow* in hue, gradually turning *greenish* on exposure, the identification

Orange-milk Agaric

Lactarius deliciosus

PLATE XVIII

THE ORANGE-MILK MUSHROOM

Lactarius deliciosus

Pileus: Diameter three to five inches. Color varying from yellow to dull orange, or even brownish yellow with mottled zones of deeper color, especially in younger plants; outline at first convex, ultimately somewhat funnel-shaped; surface usually smooth and moist.

Flesh: Brittle; creamy, more or less stained with orange.

Gills: Orange; generally clearer in hue than the pileus; when bruised, exuding a copious milky juice of orange color, becoming greenish in drying.

Stem: Paler than pileus; hollow; occasionally spotted with orange or greenish stains from bruises.

Spores: White.

Taste: Slightly peppery.

Habitat: Woods, pine-groves, and swamps.

Season: July–September.

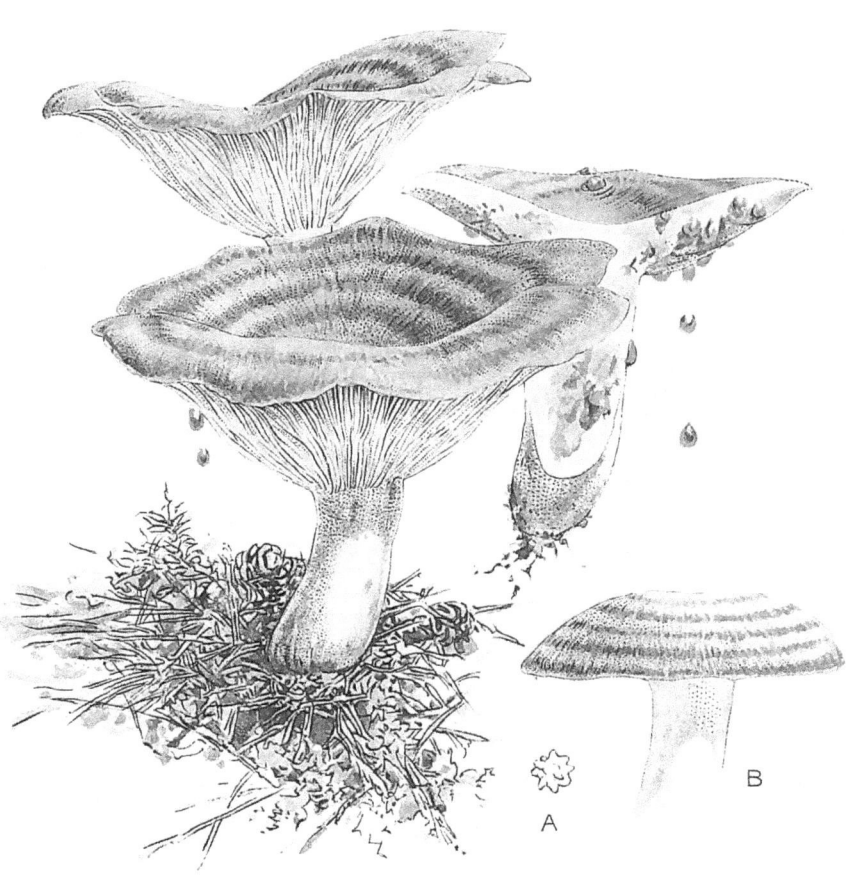

Lactarius Deliciosus

is complete, and we have the orange-milk *L. deliciosus*, of which an authority says, " It really deserves its name, being the most delicious mushroom known." W. G. Smith goes still further in its praise, assuring us that " when cooked with taste and care it is one of the greatest delicacies of the vegetable kingdom." The taste of this species when raw is slightly acrid, but this quality disappears in the cooking.

One other species of Lactarius, *L. volemum*, may properly find a place in this work as being easily recognized. In general shape it resembles *L. deliciosus*. The top is of a rich sienna golden hue; the gills are crowded.

<small>Mild white-milk species</small>

The milk is *white* as it first falls from the fracture, becoming *dull dark-reddish*, and having a mild, pleasant taste; gills white, at length yellowish or buff-colored. This species is esculent.

Other species are accounted edible, even one—the peppery Lactarius, *L. piperatus*—a pure-white variety, whose copious exudations of *white* milk will almost blister the lips, an *acrid* property which is claimed by Curtis,

<small>Peppery white-milk species</small>

Smith, and others to be dispelled in cooking, by which treatment it becomes delicious and wholesome.

This species may reach a diameter of seven inches, its shape at first rounded, convex, then flat, concave, and finally funnel-shaped, as in many of the species. But its decidedly ardent tang in the raw state, as reminiscent from my own experience, warns me not to dwell too enthusiastically upon its merits in my limited selection of desirable esculent species.

THE CHANTARELLE
Cantharellus cibarius

Bearing somewhat the shape of the Lactarius, but having its own distinguishing features, is the Chantarelle (Plate 19).

The "Agarics," as already described on page 79, are distinguished by the feature of the gills, or thin laminated curtains—the *hymenium*—upon which the spores are produced, and from which they are shed beneath the mushroom. These gills vary in thickness and number in the various species, and in one genus are so short, thick, swollen, and branched as to give rather the effect of turgid veins than gills, as shown in the accompanying sectional drawing. We occasionally come upon one of these mushrooms in our walks, usually in the woods. When it first appears the cap is rounded, and the rim folded inward towards the stem; but in mature specimens it assumes the flat or, later, the cup-shaped form shown in Plate 19.

Fluted gills

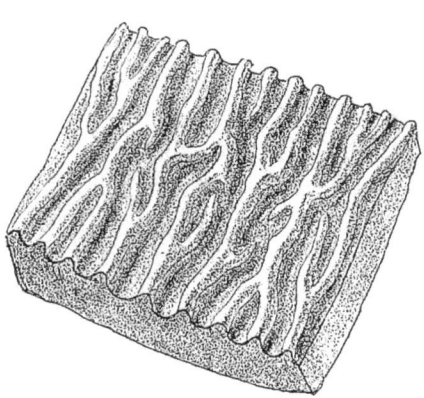

SECTION OF CHANTARELLE

A fungus thus formed is a Chantarelle, or *Cantharellus*, and is readily identified. Any specimen

Cantharellus cibarius

PLATE XIX

THE CHANTARELLE

Cantharellus cibarius

Pileus: At first convex, later flat; three to five inches in diameter, with central hollow, and finally almost funnel form. Color, bright to deep yellow above and below.

Gills: Shallow and fluted, resembling swollen veins, branched, more or less interconnected and tapering off down the stem; color same as pileus.

Stem: Solid, generally (often slightly) tapering towards base; paler than pileus or gills.

Spores: Very pale yellow ochre in color; elliptical.

Taste: Peppery and pungent in the raw state; mild and sweet after cooking.

Odor: Suggesting ripe apricots or plums.

Habitat: In woods, especially hemlocks, generally in clusters of two or three, or in lines or arcs of several individuals.

PLATE XIX

CANTHARELLUS CIBARIUS.

having these features, and which possesses in addition a fine, rich yellow color, is the *C. cibarius* of our plate, the esculent morsel so highly prized by epicures on the Continent, where to many—perhaps somewhat indiscriminating—gastronomists it forms one of the greatest delicacies among the entire list of edible fungi. The diameter of the mature specimen may reach five inches, though three inches will be nearer the average size. The cap is frequently quite eccentric in its form, wavy-edged, or even folded upon itself in occasional individuals; but the pure, deep yellow color "suggesting the yolk of an egg," and the swollen, vein-like hymenium, generally of a similar color, will be sufficient to distinguish it under any disguise of mere form. Another unique characteristic is its odor, which suggests ripe apricots or plums. The taste of the Chantarelle when raw is pungent and peppery, but this quality disappears in cooking. The spores are of a pale yellow-ochre color, and beneath the microscope are elliptical in shape.

Botanical characters

From the last of May until early November the Chantarelle may be found in our woods, with more or less frequency, singly or in clusters. According to Dr. Badham, an eminent authority on esculent fungi, "the best ways of dressing the Chantarelle are to stew or mince it by itself, or to combine it with meat or with other fungi. It requires long and gentle stewing to make it tender, but by soaking it in milk the night before, less cooking will be requisite."

Stewed Chantarelle

But the recipes employed in Great Britain and upon the Continent to the glory of the Chantarelle would almost fill a fair-sized receipt book, and some of them are quite elaborate. A few of these are given in a later chapter. After a trial of a number of them the writer is assured that the simple broiling or frying in butter or oil, with proper seasoning, and serving on toast, will prove a most acceptable substitute.

Another species of Chantarelle, which might possibly be confounded with the *C. cibarius*, is the Orange Chantarelle, *C. aurantiacus*, which is **Another species** pronounced "scarcely esculent" by the authorities. Its average size is much smaller than the true Chantarelle, and its much deeper orange hue, and straighter, more regularly branched and crowded gills, will readily identify it, the gills of *cibarius* being thicker, and usually somewhat eccentric and netted. Like the foregoing, it assumes the funnel form with age, as indicated in the generic name, Cantharellus—"a diminutive drinking-cup."

Polyporei or Tube-bearing Fungi

Polyporei

HE previous examples of mushrooms have all been included in the order of the Agarics, or "gill-bearing" fungi, the under spore-bearing surface of the cap having been disposed in the form of laminæ or gills. We will now pass to the consideration of a class of mushrooms certain of which enjoy a wider reputation as "toadstools" than any other species, a new botanical order of fungi — the Polyporei — in which the gills are replaced by *pores* or tubes — polyporus (many pores). Conspicuous among the Polyporei are those great shelf-like woody growths so frequently to be seen on the trunks of trees, and popularly known as "punk," "tinder," and "touch-wood," and many of which increase in size year by year by accession of growth at the rim. A few of these lateral-stemmed species are edible during their young state, one or two of which are included in my subsequent pages. But the most notable group from the standpoint of esculence is the typical genus *Boletus*, containing a large number of species, and of which Plate 20 presents a conspicuous example. Especial attention should here be called to the nota-

ble monograph on the Boleti of the United States by State Botanist Professor Charles Peck, of Albany University, New York, which presents detailed descriptions of one hundred and eight indigenous species. Other contributions to mycological literature by this distinguished American authority are noted in my bibliographical list at the close of the volume.

Works by Prof. Peck

THE BOLETI
Tube mushrooms

The structure of these mushrooms is clearly shown in Plate 38, in my chapter on " Spore-prints," the hymenium being here spread upon the honey-combed pore surfaces, and shedding its spores from the tubes. Each of these tubes is distinct and may be separated from the mass.

The ideal form as shown in Plate 20 is perfectly symmetrical, in which condition the pores would naturally be perpendicular. But this perfection seldom prevails, and we continually find the specimens more or less eccentric in shape, especially where they are crowded or have met with obstruction in growth. But in any case, no matter what the angle or distortion of growth during development, the *tubes* are always adjusted to the perpendicular, or in malformed individuals as nearly so as the conditions will permit, as shown in the section on next page.

The Boleti are in general a salubrious group. Certain species have long been accredited as being poisonous, and others excluded from the feast as "suspicious." The early authorities caution us to avoid all Boleti having any shade of red on the spore-bearing surface beneath, even as it was originally claimed that all *red-capped* toadstools were poisonous. But from the writer's own individual experiments, reinforced by the experience of others, he is beginning to be persuaded that the Boletus as a *genus* has been

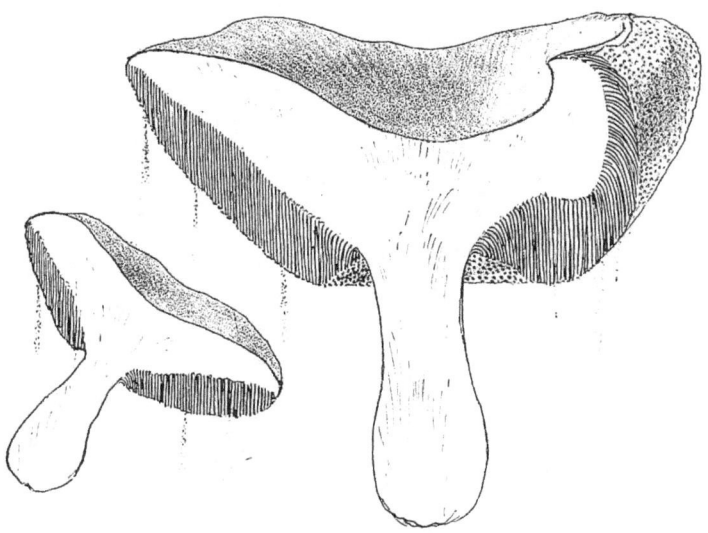

SECTION OF BOLETUS SHOWING PERPENDICULAR TUBES

maligned. Many species accredited as poisonous he has eaten repeatedly without the slightest deleterious consequences, including the crimson Boletus, *B. alveolatus* (Plate 24, fig. 2), with its red spore surface, and the *B. subtomentosus* (Plate 22, fig. 1), whose yellowish flesh, like the species just mentioned, changes quickly to blue upon fracture, a chemical feature which has long stamped both species as dangerous.

It is interesting to note that the ban is gradually being lifted from the Boleti by mycophagists of distinction, largely through their own experiments. Thus I note that Mr. McIlvaine, who has made a close study of esculent fungi, in a recent article claims that "all the Boleti are harmless, though some are too bitter to eat"; and Mr. Palmer, in his admirable portfolio of esculent fungi, includes among his edible species one of those whose flesh "changes color on fracture," and which has hitherto been proscribed as "off color." Of course, this food selection would obviously apply only to species of inviting attributes, possessing pleasant odor, agreeable taste, and delicate fibre. The selection comprised in this volume is confined to a few varieties of established good repute. As to the rest—if only on the consideration of idiosyncrasy—it is wiser to urge extreme caution on the lines laid down on page 34.

Maligned species

The Boletus, like all other mushrooms, passes through a variety of forms from its birth to maturity, at first being almost round, then convex, with the spore surface nearly flat, horizontal, the profile outline finally almost equally cushion-like on both upper and lower surfaces, or the upper surface absolutely flat. Mere outline drawings of a number of Boleti would be almost identical. The form alone, therefore, is of minor importance in their identification. Among those more readily recognized by their color and structural features, may be classed the following common species:

Changes of form in growth

Boletus edulis

PLATE XX

EDIBLE BOLETUS

Boletus edulis

Pileus: Cushion-like; moist; variable in color, light brown to darker brownish red; surface smooth but dull; dimensions at full expansion, three to six or eight inches.

Tube surface (*A*—magnified): Whitish in very young specimens, at length becoming yellow and yellowish green. Pore openings, angled.

Spores: Ochre-colored.

Stem: Stout; often disproportionately elongated. Pale brown, generally with a fine raised net-work of pink lines near junction of cap.

Flesh: White or yellowish, not changing color on fracture.

Taste: Agreeable and nutty, especially when young.

Habitat: Woods, especially during July and August; common.

PLATE XX

BOLETUS EDULIS.

EDIBLE TUBE MUSHROOM
Boletus edulis

The most prominent member of the Boleti is the typical species whose portrait I have given on Plate 20, "in vain calling himself '*edulis*,' where there were none to believe him." But in spite of this remark of Dr. Badham, which had reference especially to his native country, England, this fungus had long been a favorite article of food among a large class of the more lowly Europeans, to say nothing of the luxurious epicures of the continent.

<small>A famous delicacy</small>

Boletus edulis is to be found singly or in groups, usually in the woods. Its average diameter is perhaps four or five inches, though specimens are occasionally found of double these dimensions. A letter to the writer from a correspondent in the Rocky Mountains describes specimens measuring fifteen inches in diameter having been found there.

The cushion-liké cap is more or less convex, according to age, of a soft brownish or drab color somewhat resembling kid, and with velvety softness to the touch. The under surface or hymenium is thickly beset, honey-combed with minute vertical pores, which will leave a pretty account of themselves upon a piece of white paper laid beneath them and protected from the least draught, a process by which we may always obtain a deposit of the ochre-tinted spores, as is further described in a later chapter.

<small>Specific characters</small>

In *Boletus edulis* this pore surface is white in young specimens, later yellow, finally becoming bright olive-green; flesh *white* or *creamy*, unchangeable on fracture. Stem paler than cap, thick, swollen at base, often malformed and elongated, especially when from a cluster, generally more or less covered with vertical raised ridges, which become somewhat netted together and pinkish as they approach the cap. The taste is sweet, and in the very young specimen, which is brittle, quite suggestive of raw chestnut.

Any Boletus answering this description may be eaten without fear, assuming, of course, that its substance is free from any taint of dissolution and traces of insect contamination. Both of these conditions are too apt to prevail in the mature specimens, and all Boleti are more safely employed for food in their young crisp stage, or at least before their full expansion. In their maturity, moreover, they often prove too mucilaginous in consistency to be pleasant to the average partaker, especially the novice.

Insects and decay

In preparing them for the table, all that is necessary is to cut off the stems, which are apt to be tough and fibrous, and to wipe the pellicle of the cap perfectly clean, or, if preferred, to pare the pileus with a very sharp knife. It is recommended by some that the entire mass of the pore section be removed. In a mature specimen this would reduce the bulk of the mushroom by half, and, moreover, deprive the remainder of the full flavor of the fun-

Preparation for table

Boletus scaber

ROUGH-STEMMED BOLETUS

Boletus scaber

Pileus: Rounded convex; diameter two to five inches; surface occasionally smooth and viscid when moist; color usually brownish red, but varying from orange brick red or even black in certain varieties to yellow or whitish.

Tube surface: Rounded, cushion-like; whitish at first, becoming dingy; tube openings small and round, and rather long as seen in section.

Spores: Reddish brown.

Stem: Solid, dingy white, tapering slightly above, more or less thickly beset with brownish, fibrous, dot-like scales, this being the most pronounced botanical character for identification.

Flesh: White or dingy in certain varieties, often changing to blue, brown, pinkish, or black where wounded.

Taste: Negatively pleasant.

Habitat: A common and widely distributed species, with many variations of color. Found in woods and shaded waste-places.

Season: July–October.

PLATE XXI

BOLETUS SCABER.

gus. I have not found it necessary, and it is certainly needless in a young and tender specimen.

ROUGH-STEMMED BOLETUS
Boletus scaber

This is a very common mushroom in our woods all through the summer and autumn, in reasonably moist weather. It is figured in Plate 21. The cap of an average specimen expands four inches or more, is of a brown or brownish buff color, and viscid when moist. The pore-surface is *dingy white*, the *tube* orifices being quite *minute* and *round*—not so conspicuously angular or honey-combed as in other species—and with occasional reddish stains, presumably a deposit from the floating *spores*, which are *tawny reddish*. The flesh is dirty white, the stem solid, contracting upwards, and rough with fibrous *brownish scaly* points—whence the name "*scaber*"—often arranged somewhat in vertical lines. Epicures fail to agree as to the esculent qualities of this mushroom. It is certainly inferior to the *edulis*.

THE YELLOW-CRACKED BOLETUS
Boletus subtomentosus

The general contour of the present species — *B. subtomentosus* (Plate 22, fig. 1)—resembles the foregoing, but it is easily distinguished by the color of its cap and tube surface, the pileus being usually olive, olive-brown, or red of various shades; the color, however, does not extend to the flesh beneath the peeled cuticle, as in *B. chrysenteron*, Fig. 2. The

Specific qualities

surface is soft and dry—subtomentous—to the touch. Cracks in the cap become yellow, on which account this species is called the "yellow-cracked Boletus," in contradistinction to the red-cracked *B. chrysenteron*. Its most important distinction, however, is of a chemical nature.

The stem is stout, unequal, firm, yellowish, and more or less ribbed, occasionally tinted, minutely dotted, or faintly striped with the color of the cap. The taste of the flesh is sweet and agreeable. Palmer compares it to the flavor of walnuts. The tube surface is *yellow or yellowish green*, and the *tubes and yellowish flesh of cap and stem turn a rich peacock-blue immediately on fracture, becoming deeper* moment by moment until the entire exposed portion becomes leaden — especially noticeable in mature specimens. The pore surface shows a similar blue stain whenever bruised. The tubes are angular-sided instead of round, and much larger than in the *B. edulis;* spores ochre colored.

<small>The blue stain</small>

This blue stain was formerly, and is even now, deemed sufficient with many mycophagists to place this mushroom on the black-list, but is believed by Mr. Palmer and Mr. McIlvaine to be unwarranted as a stigma, assuming that fresh specimens are employed. The *B. subtomentosus* is also among the eleven edible Boleti in the list of Dr. Curtis, given on a previous page, and the present author has habitually eaten the species with enjoyment and without unpleasant results. Fresh young specimens

<small>An unwarranted stigma</small>

Boletus subtomentosus

Boletus chrysenteron

PLATE XXII

YELLOW CRACKED BOLETUS

1. Boletus subtomentosus

Pileus: Diameter three to six inches. Color, varying in different individuals, yellowish brown, olive, or subdued tan color; epidermis soft and dry, with a fine pubescence. Cracks in surface become yellow.

Flesh: Creamy white in mature specimens, changing to blue, and at length leaden on fracture.

Tube surface: Yellow or yellowish green, becoming bluish when bruised; opening of tubes large and angled.

Stem: Stout; yellowish; minutely roughened with scurfy dots, or faintly striped with brown.

Spores: Brownish ochre.

Taste: Sweet and agreeable.

Habitat: Woods.

Season: Summer and autumn.

GOLDEN-FLESH BOLETUS

2. Boletus chrysenteron

Pileus: Diameter two to four inches; convex, becoming more flattened; soft to the touch, varying from light yellowish brown to bright brick red; more or less fissured with red cracks and clincks.

Flesh: Rich, bright yellow, red immediately beneath the cuticle.

Tube surface: Olive-yellow, becoming bluish where bruised; tube openings rather large, angled, and unequal in size.

Stem: Generally stout and straight; yellowish, and more or less streaked or spotted with the color of the cap.

Spores: Light brown.

Habitat: Woods and copses.

Season: Summer and autumn.

Boletus Subtomentosus B Chrysenteron

with the least change of color would perhaps be the wiser choice for the novice.

Another species having this peculiar property of "turning blue" even in a more marked degree, and named, in consequence, the *B. cyanescens*, though always heretofore considered poisonous, is now pronounced by certain prominent mycophagists to be not only harmless but esculent. It is still advisable, however, to caution moderation in its use as food, if only on the ground of idiosyncrasy. The spores of this species are *white*, which, with the more minute tube openings, form a sufficient discrimination from *subtomentosus*. The spores should be obtained by a deposit on black or dark-colored paper. The flesh is white also. Other blue-stain species, such as *B. alveolatus* (Plate 24), are still considered with suspicion, presumably groundless.

Caution advisable

YELLOW-FLESHED BOLETUS
Boletus chrysenteron

Among the toadstools which tradition would surely brand as poisonous on account of "bright color" is the common species whose name heads this paragraph, and which is illustrated in Plate 22, fig. 2. In its various shapes it suggests the preceding varieties. Its cap, however, is brownish red, often bright *brick red*. *Flesh almost lemon-yellow*, stained *red just beneath* the cuticle, and *not noticeably changeable* on fracture. *Tube surface yellowish green*, turning blue or bluish green when bruised. Spores light brown. *Tubes* rather *large*, angular, and *unequal in shape of aperture.* Stem yellow, often brightly colored with the red of the cap. Chance cracks in its surface become red, whence the common name of the "Red-cracked Boletus." A species frequent in woods throughout the summer and autumn, and edible.

In its brightly colored cap it might possibly be superficially confounded with the suspicious *Boletus alveolatus* of Plate 24. But the latter species is easily distinguished by its rose-colored spores and red pore surface.

CONE-LIKE BOLETUS
Strobilomyces strobilaceus

Another allied species, not especially famous for its esculent qualities, but which is, nevertheless, not to be despised, is here introduced on account of its especially pronounced character (Plate 23)—the cone-like Boletus, or, more properly, Strobilomyces. It is of a brownish gray color, its shaggy surface more or less studded with deep brown or black woolly points, each at the centre of a scale-like segment. The tubes beneath are covered by the veil in the younger specimens, but this at length breaks, leaving ragged fragments hanging from the rim of the pileus. The pore surface thus exposed is at first a grayish white, ultimately becoming brown. The substance of the fungus turns red when broken or cut.

Botanical characters

This very striking mushroom is found in woods, especially under evergreens. It frequently attains a diameter of four inches. Its spores are a deep brown, and a specimen selected at the stage when the

Strobilomyces strobilaceus

PLATE XXIII

THE CONE-LIKE BOLETUS

Strobilomyces strobilaceus

Pileus: From two to four inches in diameter, covered with a soft gray wool drawn into regular cone-like points tipped with dark brown.
Flesh grayish white, turning red when bruised.

Pore surface: Grayish white in young specimen, and then usually covered with the veil; dark brown or almost black at maturity. Plate 38 shows a spore-print of this species.

Spores: Very dark brown.

Taste: Negatively pleasant.

Odor: Sweet and mild.

Habitat: Woods; singly or in small clusters.

PLATE XXII

STROBILOMYCES STROBILACEUS.

under surface is *flat* will yield a most beautiful spore print if laid upon white paper and protected from the atmosphere, as described in a later chapter.

A reproduction of one of these prints is shown in Plate 38, the white reticulation representing the contact of the tube orifices with the paper, each tube depositing its dot composed of spores, the depth of color increasing in proportion to the time involved in the deposit. A single mushroom will yield a half-dozen or more prints. This fungus dries readily, and may be kept indefinitely.

Black spore=prints

SUSPICIOUS BOLETI
Boletus felleus—B. alveolatus

In Plate 24 are shown two examples of the Boleti which have commonly been accounted poisonous— *B. felleus* and *B. alveolatus*—and, in the absence of absolutely satisfactory assurance to the contrary, it is safer from our present point of view to consider them still as suspicious and to give them a wide berth. There can be no doubt but that the popular condemnation of the Boleti has been altogether too sweeping. The gradual accession of many questionable species to the edible list of Messrs. McIlvaine and Palmer and other daring mycophagists is a sufficient attestation of this fact. Thus *subtomentosus* and *cyanescens*, already described, always heretofore branded as reprobates, are now redeemed from obloquy, and even the universal ill-repute of the *B. satanas*, with its pale pileus and blood-red pores,

Maligned species

has not frightened the indefatigable Captain McIlvaine from a personal challenge and encounter with this lurid specimen, with the result that the formidable "Satanas" has proved anything but deserving of its name—not half so lurid as it has been painted; indeed, it has been even pronounced "the best of them all." Of course there's no telling to what extent the considerations of contrast, through surprise and the consequent demoralization on the contingents of the personal equation, may have influenced the captain's discrimination, but it certainly would appear, to put it negatively, that even the ill-favored world-renowned *B. satanas* has apparently been freed from aspersion as an enemy of mankind.

A daring pioneer mycophagist

But it is well for the amateur to avoid these notorious species absolutely until their edibility becomes universally accepted by the "professionals."

The *Boletus felleus* (Plate 24, fig. 1) is a very common species. The pinkish substance of this Boletus is so extremely bitter when raw as to make it sufficiently repellent as food. The color of its smooth cap varies from creamy yellow to reddish brown. Substance white in young specimens, flesh color or pinkish in older individuals. Tube surface white at first, becoming pinkish. Opening of tubes, angled. Stem usually more or less netted with raised lines towards cap. Spores pinkish or "flesh colored." Common in rich soil in woods.

The bitter Boletus

Boletus alveolatus. — Pileus smooth and polished, usually rich crimson or maroon, sometimes varied

Boletus alveolatus
Boletus felleus

PLATE XXIV

SUSPICIOUS BOLETI

Alveolate Boletus—Boletus alveolatus

Pileus: Smooth, polished; bright, deep crimson or maroon, occasionally mottled or marbled with yellowish; three to six inches in diameter.

Flesh: Firm and solid in substance; pale greenish or yellowish white, changing blue in fracture or where bruised.

Tubes: Tube-surface reaching the stem proper; undulate with uneven hollows; maroon, the tubes in section being yellow beyond their dark red mouths.

Spores: Yellowish brown.

Stem: Usually disproportionately long, covered with depressions or oblong pitted indentations, with intermediate coarse network of raised ridges; red and yellow.

Habitat: Woods; quite common.

Bitter Boletus—Boletus felleus

Pileus: At first firm in substance, becoming soft and cushion-like; smooth, without polish, varying in color from pale ochre to yellowish or reddish brown; diameter three to nine inches.

Flesh: White on immediate section, generally changing to slight pinkish or flesh color in fracture.

Tubes: Tube-surface rounded upward as it reaches stem; white at first, becoming dull pinkish with age, or upon being bruised.

Spores: Flesh colored or dull pink.

Stem: Usually quite stout, nearly as smooth as the cap, and somewhat lighter in color; more or less ridged with coarse reticulations, occasionally covered with them to its thickened base.

Taste: Bitter.

Habitat: Rich woods and copses, often about decaying trunks.

PLATE XXIV

Suspicious Boleti.
BOLETUS ALVEOLATUS.   B. FELLEUS.

with paler yellowish tints. Substance very solid, changing to blue on fracture or bruise. Tube surface deep dull crimson or maroon, this color not extending the full length of the pores, which are yellow a short distance above their mouths. The stem is quite stout and tall for the size of the cap as compared with other Boleti. It is mottled in yellow and bright red or crimson, and conspicuously meshed with a net-work of firm ridges. The spores are yellowish brown. A conspicuous and easily identified species.

The crimson Boletus

THE VEGETABLE BEEFSTEAK
Fistulina hepatica

Our next member of the Polyporus order, or tube-bearing fungi, is a unique member of the fungus tribe, and cannot be mistaken for any other species. An example of this species is shown in Plate 25, the *beefsteak* mushroom — *Fistulina hepatica*. The specimen from which my drawing was made was found growing at the foot of a chestnut-tree, and was about nine inches across by about two in greatest thickness. Its upper surface was dark meaty red or liver colored, somewhat wet, or viscid and clammy, and its taste slightly acid. The under tube surface was yellowish white, and, as the section will show, was proportionately thin—the pores being about one-eighth of an inch in length. The solid red substance much resembled meat, and in sections was streaked with darker lines of red, as indicated in plate, somewhat suggesting a section of beet-root.

Botanical characters

Though not common in my vicinity, I nevertheless succeed in obtaining a few specimens during the season. It varies greatly in size and shape. M. C. Cooke, in his admirable "plain and easy" account of British fungi, says of it: "When old it affords an excellent gravy, and when young, if sliced and grilled, would pass for a good beefsteak. Specimens are now and then met with that would furnish four or five men with a good dinner, and they have been collected weighing as much as thirty pounds. The liver, or paler pinkish meaty color, clammy viscidity, and streaky section are sufficient guides in the recognition of this species."

<small>Savory qualities</small>

It is a highly prized article of diet on the Continent where the arts of the chef are ingeniously employed in endless recipes for its savory preparation, often, it would seem, with the main object of obliterating as far as possible all trace of the delicate flavor of the mushroom *per se*.

<small>Culinary preparation</small>

If the reader's experience correspond with the writer's in his mycological experiments "*à la mode*," he will gladly fall back to the plain plebeian method of simply broiling over the coals, or frying or roasting in the pan, with the least possible seasoning of pepper, salt, and butter, relying upon his mushroom to furnish the predominant zest and flavor.

Other hints for serving this fungus are given in a later chapter. Besides the common name of "beefsteak mushroom," it is also known on the Continent as the "oak tongue," and "chestnut tongue."

Fistulina hepatica

PLATE XXV

THE BEEFSTEAK MUSHROOM

Fistulina hepatica

Pileus: Diameter, average specimen, about six inches, occasionally twice or three times this size; color varying from pinkish to dark meaty red; surface roughened with minute papillæ; soft and moist.

Flesh: Light red, streaked with darker red; tender and juicy in young specimens; juice light red.

Tube surface: Creamy in color; tubes distinct from each other, crowded, very short, as shown in section opposite.

Stem: Short or obsolete, growing at the side.

Taste: Slightly acid.

Habitat: On the stumps and trunks of oak and chestnut trees.

Season: July–September.

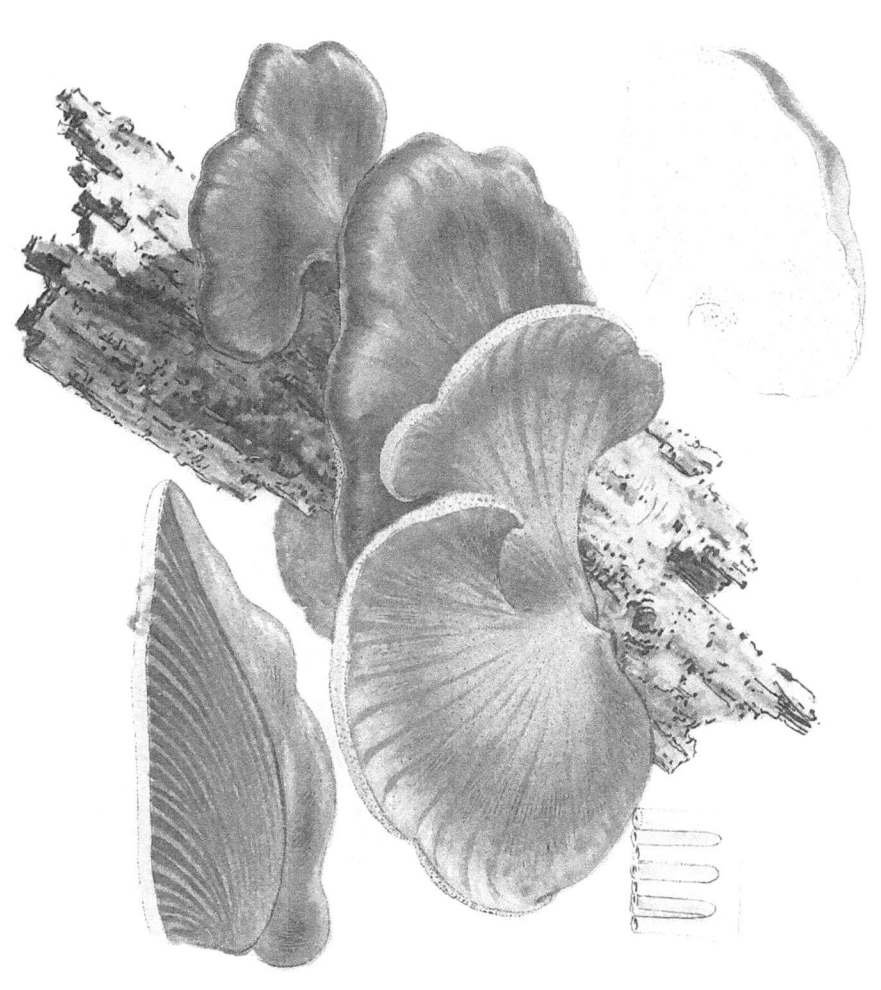

THE SULPHUROUS POLYPORUS
Polyporus sulphureus

Probably the most conspicuous member of our native polyporei remains to be considered among the esculents, though until recently it was included in the black list, Dr. Curtis, of North Carolina, I believe, having first demonstrated its edibility, though pronouncing it merely "tolerable."

The brilliancy of its sulphur-yellow and orange-salmon colors, in association with its large size, renders it a most conspicuous object, especially from its

habit of growing in dense clusters, often a number of such clusters in close contiguity upon a decaying stump or prostrate log, frequently so numerous and so crowded as to completely conceal the bark beneath, as shown in the accompanying figure, or completely covering a space of several square feet.

There lies before me even as I write a fragment of a single cluster which I plucked yesterday from the trunk of an apparently healthy red-oak near my studio, the remainder of the clump having been enjoyed as a special course in my dinner of last evening. In Plate 26 I present a portrait of this specimen, the well-named Sulphur Polyporus — *Polyporus sulphureus*. It may be found frequently from July till frost upon its favorite habitat of old trunk, stump, log water-trough, or fence-post, usually upon wood in the early stages of decay. A single cluster will often measure a foot in diameter through its very solid mass of thickened pulpy branches, its early and esculent stage being thus compact with the subdivisions ascending from their common thick stem, the mass somewhat suggesting a cauliflower in shape, as shown in the illustration above.

A YOUNG SPECIMEN

The general color at this tender stage is pure sulphur-yellow, this being the ultimate *lower* or spore surface now exposed by its upright position. The true upper surface or cap of the later eccentrically branched fungus is of a bright orange-salmon color, and is mostly concealed by the crowded growth.

The specimen above alluded to would have weighed about two pounds, and this central mass was so crowded as to afford scarcely a glimpse of the pinkish-orange pileus surface. Upon showing my specimen to a friend, I was informed that a certain log by the roadside about two miles distant was covered with this same kind of fungus, which seemed to be spreading all over the ground. Doubtless ten or twenty pounds of good nourishing food was thus going begging by the way-side, even in sight of a rural homestead, whose lord and master finds the butcher's bill a serious drain upon his resources.

<small>A voice in the wilderness</small>

My plate shows a more open cluster of the fungus in its earlier stages, the *only* time when it is fit for food. In this condition it is tender, succulent, and juicy. In a few days the lobed fringes or fan-like divisions have lowered and spread out as widely as their crowded condition will permit, assuming the horizontal or even drooping position seen at C, and at D in the plate, as viewed from above. The pileus now being exposed, the fungus presents a deep orange-red or salmon color to the beholder, its sulphurous-hued pore surface being turned beneath. Its texture at this adult stage is tough, fibrous, and almost woody, especially as it approaches the stem, and no one would think of eating it.

The young specimen, however, is quite delicious and wholesome, and, considering that a single cluster will afford a dinner for a large family, its importance as a food product, especially to the farmer or peasant who finds economy a necessity, is thus manifest.

Tasted at the tip, it yields for the first moment of mastication an acid flavor recalling that of the *Fistulina hepatica*. This is followed by a sweet, slightly mucilaginous savor, which, in the realization that the species is wholesome, will at once prove an invitation to further experiment with the fungus as food.

The texture of the young mushroom will be found to vary in its different parts, extremely tender at the thickened tuberculated tips, becoming fibrous as the stem is approached, and increasing in toughness, in fracture suggesting wood in appearance (see A, Plate 26), and unless the specimen is *very* young this portion will have to be excluded from the diet. Excepting this precaution it needs no preparation for the table, assuming, of course, that the substance is free from grubs, which will presumably be the case, as I have never seen this fungus thus infested except in its more advanced woody growth.

Texture and quality

I have not as yet satisfied myself as to the best methods of cooking this polyporus. Fried in butter it has a tendency to become slightly tough in consistency, in its white stringy fibre as well as in taste closely suggesting the "white meat" of chicken. It lends itself well to a stew or ragoût, and might, perhaps, to a curry, the substance being cut or broken in small pieces and treated after the manner of meat under similar recipes. Following the hints contained in our last chapter, many methods of its culinary treatment will suggest themselves.

Methods of cooking

The freely expanded specimen of this species is

Polyporus sulphureus

PLATE XXVI

THE SULPHUROUS POLYPORUS

Polyporus sulphureus

In the mature specimen the growth is horizontal, spreading fan-like from stem, undulating with radiating flutings. Upper surface salmon orange or orange red, the edge being smooth and unevenly thickened with nodule-like prominences. In young specimen ascending, under yellow surface outwardly exposed.

Pore Surface: Bright sulphur yellow; pores very minute.

Spores: Dingy white.

Stem: Very short; a mere close attachment for the spreading growth.

Taste: Slightly acid and mucilaginous when raw; after cooking somewhat suggesting white meat of chicken.

Odor: Suggesting *A. campestris*.

Habitat: On tree trunks, particularly oaks, often growing in very large clusters.

A. Section of fungus showing fibre.
C. and *D*. Matured specimen.

PLATE XXV

Polyporus Sulphureus

full of beauty, in its wavy fan-like form and flowing lines and flutings presenting a suggestive decorative theme, whether in the branches of painting, sculpture, or the plastic arts. The pores upon its sulphurous surface are so minute as to be scarcely visible, but they shed a copious quantity of whitish spores. The pileus of the dried specimen is often more or less frosted with minute white crystals— binoxalate of potash — and the spore surface dulls to the color of buckskin.

Its ornamental attributes

Another remarkable feature about this fungus, if report be true, is its visibility by night, not merely from its pale yellow hue, but by an actual flood of bluish luminous phosphorescent light, the environment of its haunt in the woods sometimes being lighted up by the effulgence from its ample mass of growth, a resource not uncommon among the fungi, and popularly known under the name of "foxfire." This phenomenon is frequently observable in woods at night, following rainy weather. An old stump or prostrate log will appear streaked with lines of brilliant light. If we approach and detach the loosened bark, its back and the decayed surface of the log thus exposed will prove ablaze in phosphorescence, whose presence had scarcely been suspected but for the chance fissures which revealed the telltale streaks. I recall from my boyhood experience one such midnight episode as this in which, from the peculiar outline of the fallen trunk and the coincident circumstance of two approximate dots of brill-

Luminous by night

iant light suggesting the eyes of a huge puma or tiger, I stood spell-bound with momentary fear, until I realized that the apparition was only a bugaboo after all. Approaching in the darkness, I soon laid hold of the rough head of the monster, and with a strong pull at the mass of bark of which it was composed, laid bare several square feet of blazing phosphorescence whose only hint had gleamed through those two imaginary eyes, which proved to be holes which had disclosed the hidden luminous fungus. One authority describes a single mass of this phosphorescence as extending the entire length of a prostrate trunk thirty feet long.

Hawthorne records having made good use of foxfire upon one occasion when, left in the lurch at night by a canal-boat, he procured a phosphorescent flambeau which effectually lighted his path for several miles through the otherwise impassable woods.

Miscellaneous Fungi

Miscellaneous Fungi

THE species of fungi thus far described have been confined to the two great orders of the Agarics and the Polyporei, which include the large majority of our edible mushrooms and toadstools.

The remainder of my selection in the present chapter comprises scattered examples from four other orders: Hydnei (Spine-bearers), Clavariei (Coral-fungi), and the Trichogastres (Puff-balls), all belonging to the first great division of the Sporifera. The remaining two species considered — Morel and Helvella, of the order Elvellacei — are my only representatives of the second grand cohort of the Sporidiifera, whose botanical characters are described on page 77.

In our previous examples the hymenium or spore-bearing surface has been disposed upon "gills," as in the Agarics, and on "tubes" in the Polypores. In the Hydnei group, which we will first consider, this disseminating surface is spread over *spines* or *teeth*.

The examples selected from this order are both in the typical genus Hydnum; and the object of this present book on fungi being especially the presentation of only such varieties as are conspicuously self-placarded by some distinctive marks for identification, these delicious spine-bearing or "hedgehog" mushrooms should of course be included—a genus which

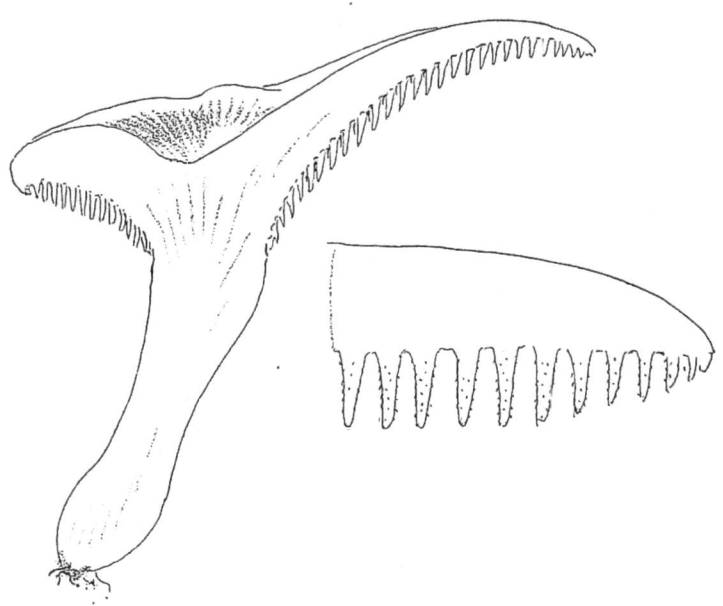

SECTION OF A HYDNUM

cannot be mistaken for any other, and which is *instantly* recognized by its own peculiar character, already mentioned, its spore surface being beset with *soft, drooping spines* instead of pores or gills. There are more than a score of species. The two more or less common with us are the *Hydnum repandum*, in outline suggesting an ordinary mushroom, and of

Нудит черандит

PLATE XXVII

THE HEDGEHOG MUSHROOM

Hydnum repandum

Pileus: Diameter two to five inches, generally irregular, with the stem off centre. Color varying from pale buff, the typical hue, to a distinct bricky red.

Spines: Beneath the cap, one-quarter to one-third inch in length; soft, creamy in tint, becoming darker in old specimens.

Flesh: Creamy white, solid.

Stem: Often set eccentrically into the cap; proportionately thick and short.

Taste: Slightly aromatic.

Habitat: Woods or shaded places in rich soil, often in clusters.

Season: Summer and autumn.

HYDNUM REPANDUM.

which the above cut represents a section, and the *H. caput-medusæ*, or Medusa-head Hydnum. None of the group is accounted poisonous, though some of them are too tough to be acceptable as food.

THE HEDGEHOG MUSHROOM
Hydnum repandum

In this species, figured on Plate 27, bearing somewhat the contour of an Agaric, the spines are all confined to the lower surface of the expanded cap. The general color of the upper surface is buff, generally very pale, occasionally almost white. The spines being of similar hue, this color and the smoothness of texture have suggested the common popular English name of "doeskin mushroom." The flesh is firm and white or creamy, turning brownish when bruised. Its sweet but slightly pungent or peppery taste when raw disappears in cooking. It is quite frequent in our woods, and if fresh and free from insects may be eaten without the slightest hesitation. It is a species highly favored on the Continent, where the surplus yield is habitually dried and kept for winter use. The hot flavor of the raw Hydnum was formerly sufficient to brand it as poisonous, Roques, I believe, having been the first to demonstrate its edibility, and Dr. Badham to distinguish its mimetic flavor—" Hydna as good as oysters, which they somewhat resemble in taste."

Characters and qualities

Cooke and Berkeley describe a variety of this mushroom having a distinctly reddish pileus—*H. rufescens*—and Prof. Charles Peck gives the species quite a range in its color gamut. " Its color may be pale buff, rusty yellow, pale red, or sienna color." The "pale buff" will doubtless be found to be the most common. In the variety *rufescens* the size is smaller and the form more symmetrical, but the general shape and fringe-toothed spore surface are sufficient to identify the typical species under any disguise of color.

<small>Variations and varieties</small>

The cap is occasionally quite symmetrical, suggesting the outline of a Boletus in profile, but more commonly is irregular and eccentric, with stem attached towards its side, as indicated in section on previous page. It may reach the diameter of five inches in a fine specimen.

Its favorite haunt is the open woods, where it may be seen from the last of June until September, either singly or in clusters, lifting the dried leaves from their bed, or occasionally barely revealed beneath them.

But the most important and savory of the entire group of Hydnei is the species following:

THE MEDUSA HYDNUM
H. caput-medusæ

While driving through the White Mountain Notch, many years ago, I chanced upon a mass of cream-colored, fringy fungus growing upon a fallen beech-log by the side of the road. The fungus was then entirely new to me, and I lost no time in making a sketch of it, with notes. The growth covered a space possibly eighteen inches wide by eight in height, and I estimated it would weigh fully five pounds, its

Hydnum caput-medusæ

PLATE XXVIII

THE MEDUSA MUSHROOM

Hydnum caput-medusæ

Spines: The long, soft spines cover the entire exposed portion of the fungus, which is disposed in fleshy branching divisions, each terminating in a "crown" of shorter, drooping teeth. The color is pale buff or dark creamy.
Stem: Short, concealed beneath the growth.
Taste: Sweet and aromatic, slightly pungent.
Habitat: Trunks of trees, especially beech.
Season: July to October.

Hydnum Caput-Medusae.

Plate XXVIII

PLATE XXIX.—HYDNUM CAPUT-MEDUSÆ

most marked feature being the dense growth of drooping spines. In my limited knowledge of edible fungi at the time, I cautiously left the specimen in the woods, afterwards to learn from Dr. Harkness, the mycologist, that I had "thrown away five pounds of the most delicious fungus meat known to the epicure." I have since found minor specimens many times, and can readily understand the enthusiastic encomiums of my connoisseur friend as to its esculent qualities.

A dinner thrown away

This species (Plate 28) cannot be confounded with any other; it is of a dark creamy color, and usually grows sidewise upon dead beech wood (Plate 29), sometimes in great profusion, especially in the summer. The soft spines entirely cover the rounded branching protuberances of the fungus. The upper teeth are short and form a sort of "crown," falling from which the more and more elongated spines are firmly pendent beneath, somewhat suggesting as many heads of tiny skye-terriers in crowded convocation —or a tiny bleached "hedgehog," if you choose.

Haunt and description

A fungus bearing such conspicuous characteristics may be gathered and eaten without fear, assuming the specimen to be fresh and free from grubs. It will be found an aromatic and savory morsel, though simply fried in butter and served on toast.

One other species may be mentioned briefly, the *H. coralloides*, or Moss-mushroom, which is unfamiliar to the writer, but which Curtis includes among his edible fungi. It may be found growing sidewise "on old trunks of living trees," *at first white*, then yellowish, resembling when young the *chou-fleur* (cauliflower). From its base, which is tender and fleshy, spring a large number of flexible branches, interlaced and assembled in tufts, bearing upon the summit of each of their divisions an expansion of long points or projections, at first straight, then pendent, and even curved under, and terminating in layers. Cordier says that it is "delicate food."

Moss-mushroom

Professor Peck speaks enthusiastically of this species. "It is found in woods, especially in hilly and mountainous districts, and occurs during rainy or showery weather from August to October. It is a pretty fungus, and very attractive to those who are neither botanists nor fungus eaters, and it is as good as it is beautiful. In our botanical expeditions in the vast wilderness of the Adirondack region, we were often obliged to camp in the woods several nights in succession. On such occasions this fungus sometimes formed a luxurious addition to our ordinarily simple and sometimes limited bill of fare."

The Hydnei may be cooked in the same manner as employed for the ordinary mushroom, or gathered and dried for winter use, a very common custom on the Continent. Owing to the somewhat firm, compact substance of these mushrooms they should be cooked *slowly*, in order to preserve their tenderness. Berkeley recommends that they be "previously" steeped in hot water. Badham especially favors the Hydnum stew, which he claims is "an excellent dish

Hydnum in the kitchen

with a flavor of oysters." According to the same authority it yields also a "very good purée." The "oyster" flavor is recognized in many of the epicurean encomiums on this species. Various hints as to its culinary treatment will be found in a later chapter.

THE CORAL OR CLUB FUNGUS
Clavaria

What frequenter of the summer and autumn woods has failed to observe that occasional dense cluster of creamy-colored, coral-like growth such as I have indicated at Plate 30, and who has thought to gather up its fragile, succulent mass with designs on the cook? I have seen clusters of this fungus so dense and ample as to strikingly suggest a huge cauliflower, and representing many pounds in weight. But in the absence of popular appreciation it must needs decay by "whole hundred-weights" in the woods.

A neglected feast

This is the Clavaria, or coral fungus—more literally translated, though less appropriate to this particular species, "club fungus"—a representative of a genus containing many edible species.

The one presented in the Plate is *Clavaria formosa*, or the elegant Clavaria. It grows from four to six inches in height, is deep creamy yellow or pale orange buff in color, and slightly reddish at tips of branches. It has a sweet taste, a fragile, brittle consistency, and white substance; its spores are pale-ochre colored. Curtis gives thirteen edible native species. Among them are the following, which hardly call for severe technical description, as the entire group are doubtless edible:

The *true* "coral fungus"—*Clavaria coralloides*—of our woods resembles *C. formosa* in general shape,

THE WHITE CORAL FUNGUS

but its color is *white*, or perhaps pale gray. Its thick stem is hollow, and its uneven, crowded branches are brittle and flesh-white. Its odor is like that of the *Agaricus campestris*, and it possesses a sweet, pleasant flavor. Cordier recommends it as eatable even when raw. This species is in great favor in Germany, Switzerland, and Italy, where it is desiccated for winter use.

Clavaria
coralloides

Clavaria formosa

PLATE XXX

THE CORAL FUNGUS

Clavaria formosa

Thickly branched from a stout pale base, the dense branchlets being tipped with two or three minute teeth.
Color: Saffron yellow. Tips generally darker and more rosy.
Flesh: White.
Spores: Ochre-tinted.
Taste: Sweet, tender, and delicate.
Height: Four to six inches.
Habitat: Woods.

PLATE XXX

CLAVARIA FORMOSA.

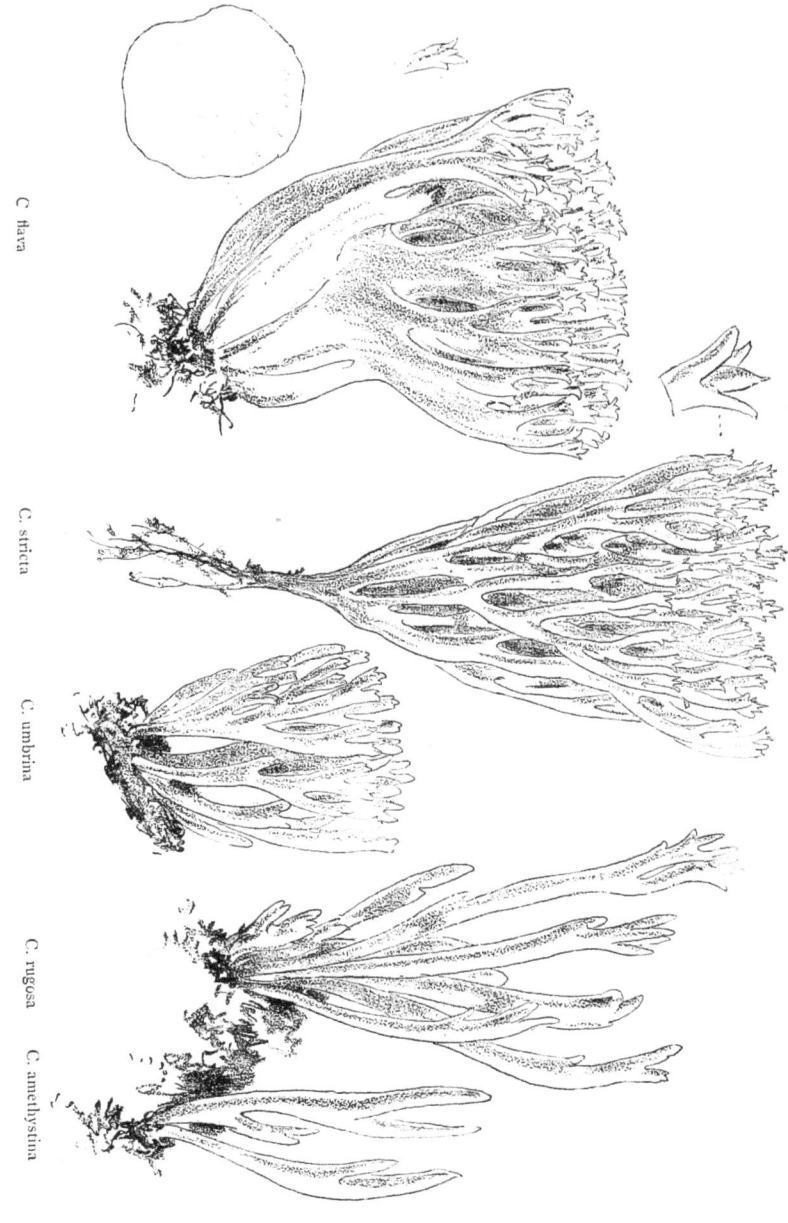

PLATE XXXI.—VARIOUS FORMS OF CLAVARIA

C. flava   C. stricta   C. umbrina   C. rugosa   C. amethystina

Clavaria fastigiata is a somewhat dwarf variety, usually found on lawns and pastures, seldom reaching a height of more than two inches. In general aspect it resembles Fig. 3 in Plate 31. It is of a yellow color, very densely branched from its short, slender stem close to the ground, the branches mostly terminating at the same height.

<small>Clavaria fastigiata</small>

All of the above-mentioned species, except *C. formosa*, have *white spores*, and while none of the genus is considered poisonous, though some are so bitter and of such tough consistency as to make them unfit for food, it is generally conceded among the authorities that *all white-spored* Clavarias *are certainly edible*. The spores are easily obtained by simply laying the fungus upon a dark surface and excluding the air, as directed in a later chapter.

<small>White-spored species edible</small>

The various forms assumed by the Clavarei are indicated in Plate 31.

Fig. 1 is *C. flava;* 2. *C. stricta;* 3. *C. umbrina;* 4. *C. rugosa;* 5. *C. amethystina*. Any specimen bearing resemblance to any of these in form, and which is found to have *white* spores, may be eaten without fear.

The Clavaria forms a most inviting relish by the simple process of frying in butter, with seasoning to taste. They have the advantage of being quite free from "fungus-worms," and in the larger species are occasionally so plentiful that a half-bushel may be gathered in a few moments.

Another species bearing the general shape suggested in Plate 31, fig. 1, is the *C. botrytis*. It has a thick, fleshy trunk and swollen branches. Its substance is very brittle; color creamy-yellow, with red-tipped branchlets. It is found in woods.

THE MOREL
Morchella esculenta

In decided contrast to any of the foregoing fungi, and of unmistakable aspect, is the famous Morel, *Morchella esculenta* (Plate 32).

The Morel belongs to a cohort of fungi known as the Sporidiifera, in which the spores are *enclosed in bag-like envelopes*, in distinction to the Sporifera, in which the spores are *naked* and *exposed*, as shown in Plates 35 and 36. These cysts, or bags, or *asci*, which resemble the *cystidium* in Plate 35, and in the family of Ascomycetes, to which the Morel belongs, each contains about eight spores, which are finally liberated by the bursting of the tip of the bag, after the manner of a Puff-ball.

Botanical characters

In the Morel the hymenium or spore-bearing surface is crowded with these cysts, and covers the entire exposed conical and pitted surface of the mushroom.

Description is hardly necessary with its portrait before us. No other fungus at all resembles it except those of the same genus, and inasmuch as they are *all edible*, we may safely add to our bill of fare any fungus which resembles our illustration. The Morel has long been considered as one of the rarest of delicacies, always at a fancy premium in the

Morchella esculenta

PLATE XXXII

THE MOREL

Morchella esculenta

Pileus: Oval, elliptical, or round in outline; diameter one inch to three inches in a large specimen; hollow. Color pale yellowish brown, varying to greenish; surface more or less regularly honeycombed with deep depressions.
Stem: Hollow, dingy white, united to the base of pileus.
Taste: Sweet and pleasant.
Habitat: Woods, orchards, and shaded grassy places.
Season: May and June.

PLATE XXXII

MORCHELLA ESCULENTA.

markets—a *bon-mot* for the rich, a prize for the peasant. I could fill all my allotted space with the delicate schemes of the chefs in its preparation for the table.

Dr. Badham's recommendation, among my list of recipes, is worth a trial for the sake of novelty, if nothing more. The hollow shape of our Morel thus suggests a variation on the conventional methods of cooking.

The color of the Morel in its prime is grayish-green, occasionally brownish. It is most commonly found in orchards, and is said to favor spots where charcoal or cinders have been thrown.

HELVELLA
Helvella crispa

One of the most strikingly individual of all the mushrooms, and one which could not possibly be confounded with any other kind, is the example pictured in Plate 33. With this mere portrait as our guide, we might safely classify our specimen—at least, as to its genus; and inasmuch as no one of the group is poisonous, and all are edible with varying degrees of esculence, we can make no mistake even in our ventures as amateur mycophagists. When, therefore, we find a fungus with such a peculiar, irregularly fluted and hollowed stem, itself hollow within, or tubular, and surmounted with a rather thin, flexible, wavy cap, resembling our illustration, we may know that we have a specimen of Helvella. If this example happens to be creamy above and ochre-colored beneath, it is the *Helvella crispa* of our Plate. The specimen here shown is somewhat larger than in nature. Other species are differently formed and colored, one of them having the cap dark ash-colored or even black. There are three species occasionally met with, of which the first, *H. crispa*, is the most common and perhaps the most delectable.

The peculiar texture of these mushrooms permits of their ready desiccation, and in Britain and on the Continent they are commonly strung on strings and dried for future use, in which condition they have been compared to dried "wash-leather" in texture.

Dried mushrooms The famous aristocratic Morel (*Morchella esculenta*), already described, so prized as food in Europe, and to which the Helvella is closely allied, has a similar irregular, pitted, hollowed, and netted surface over its entire conical or globular gray cap, and the same texture. Most competent judges claim that the delicious Morel possesses no advantages over the more plebeian Helvella as a delicacy for the table. The flavor is identical, and the other qualities of the two mushrooms make them equally desirable.

The readiness with which they may be dried, and thus kept indefinitely, is another distinct advantage which the Morels and Helvellas possess over the ordinary gilled Agarics, many of which must be gathered in their young prime and immediately eaten.

There are numerous ways of serving these fungi, among which is the common method of frying with butter or oil, and variously seasoning with onion,

Helvella crispa

PLATE XXXIII

THE WHITE HELVELLA

Helvella crispa

Pileus: Two to three inches in diameter; wavy or curled, reflexed at edges, often puckered towards centre; white or pale creamy; somewhat leathery in texture in older specimens.

Spore surface: On underside of cap, ochraceous.

Stem: White, more or less furrowed with vertical hollows.

Taste: Similar to Morel, to which it is closely allied.

Habitat: Woods.

Season: Summer and autumn.

PLATE XXXIII

HELVELLA CRISPA.

garlic, herbs, etc., according to taste, and serving on toast, or with crisped bread-crumbs. Our chapter on recipes will suggest other more elaborate methods.

PUFF-BALLS
Lycoperdaceæ

A detailed discrimination of the Puff-balls is hardly necessary here, and I will therefore omit it. While I am not inclined to go so far as to contend, as was the quaint habit of old Dr. Culpeper, in his *Herbal*, in which he was wont similarly to elude description of an herb, affirming that "he were a fool indeed who does not know this plant"—or words of similar

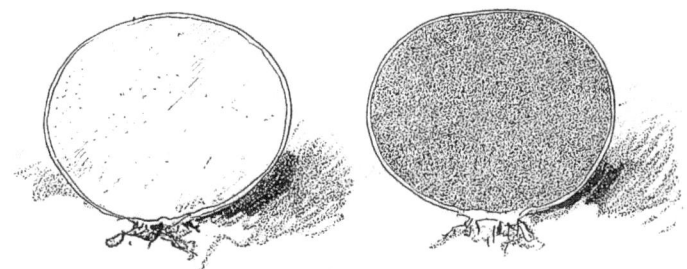

SECTION OF PUFF-BALL—Earlier and Later Stages

import—it is perfectly safe to say that if there is one fungus more than another with which the populace is *specifically* familiar it is the Puff-ball.

In these fungi, of which there are many species, the spores are incased within the white or dingy peridium or more or less globular case—*gasteromycetæ*, from *gaster*, a stomach. The interior spore substance is at first white and firm in structure, at length peppered with gray, both conditions being indicated in accompanying cut, and ultimately black or brown, after which the outer case becomes dry and papery, and soon bursts at the summit, liberating its clouds of spores with the slightest zephyr, or, later, becoming dislodged from its slender anchorage to the soil, is whisked before the breeze enveloped in its spore-smoke. Fries, the eminent fungologist, has reckoned the number of these spores in a single Puff-ball at ten millions — presumably a conservative estimate.

Spore=cloud dissemination

But it will surprise most people to know that the plebeian Puff-ball of our pastures is good for something besides the kick of the small boy.

There are a number of species of the Puff-ball, and none of them is known to be poisonous.

I have indicated an arbitrary group in Plate 34 ranging in shape and size from the small white globular variety of an inch in diameter, *L. saccatum*, and the pear-shaped *L. gemmatum*, to the giant pasture species, which may frequently attain the dimensions of a foot-ball or a bushel basket. In its larger dimensions it is more spreading in shape, being somewhat wider than high. *All the Puff-balls are edible* if gathered at the *white stage* — *i.e.*, white pulp; those of yellow or darker fracture being excluded, as the fungus in this later stage is not considered fit for food.

Various species

Of the esculent qualities of the larger species, *Lycoperdon giganteum*, we may judge from the statement

A group of Puff-balls

PLATE XXXIV

A GROUP OF PUFF-BALLS

Lycoperdaceæ

The group opposite represents three species. The largest, *L. giganteum;* the pear-shaped, *L. gemmatum;* and the small, round *L. saccatum.*

L. giganteum. The largest species. Diameter ten to twenty-five inches; often more spreading in shape than specimen shown; surface smooth; stem hardly apparent; color dingy white in the edible state, at which time the solid flesh is also white. Spore dust, at maturity, yellowish brown. Grows in fields and pastures.

L. gemmatum. Stem prolonged and tapering from above, suggesting the specific name pear-shaped; color dingy white; surface covered with deciduous warts; substance, young state, white; spore dust brown; height two to three inches.

L. saccatum. Stemless; white; setting close to the ground; one to two inches in diameter; surface covered with loose, warty granules; substance, young state, white; spore dust brown.

These and all other Puff-balls are edible in the young condition when the pulp is white.

PLATE XXXIV

A GROUP OF PUFF-BALLS.

LYCOPERDON GIGANTEUM   L. GEMMATUM.   L. SACCATUM.

of a connoisseur: "Sliced and seasoned in butter and salt, and fried in the pan, no French omelette is half as good in richness and delicacy of flavor." M. C. Cooke, the British authority, says of it: "In its young and pulpy condition it is excellent eating, and indeed has but few competitors for the place of honor at the table." Other epicurean suggestions will be found in a later page. Occasionally in its plenitude, especially during August and September, single clusters will be found which would afford a meal for a large family.

<small>Esculent qualities</small>

Other species, more or less frequent, are the *L. separans*, whose outer epidermis cracks off in flakes at maturity; *L. cyathiforme*, or cup-shaped Lycoperdon, a large species with distinctly purplish smoke so familiar to us all, the final cup-shaped remnant of its case having suggested its name. The larger specimens will be found the more fully flavored.

There is but one danger which would seem to be possible with reference to the use of the Puff-ball as food within the restrictions already given, and that is, the remote contingency—assumable only on the supposition of most careless observation—of confounding the white ball with the globular condition of the Amanita (see Plate 2, fig. 1), or other fungi of the same deadly group, which are similarly enclosed in a spherical volva in their early stages.

<small>Closing words of caution</small>

But inasmuch as this spherical period of the Amanita is usually spent underground and out of sight, and the merest glance at its contents would at once reveal the folded form of the enclosed mushroom, it would hardly seem necessary to warn the intelligent reader. But "once warned, twice armed;" and for absolute safety the tyro would do well to open every specimen, and be sure of its even, white, homogeneous substance before turning it over to the cook.

There are a number of other esculent species of fungi as easily available and enjoyable as those already described, but the scheme of the volume would hardly warrant their inclusion. Even though the element of danger is practically eliminated, so far as the identification of the foregoing fungi is concerned, it is still wise for the amateur to proceed with caution until he has absolutely *learned* the individual species in their various forms of development.

Spore-prints

Mushroom Spore-prints

OUR common dusty Puff-ball, floating its faint trail of smoke in the breeze from the ragged flue at its dome-shaped roof as from an elfin tepee, or perhaps enveloping our feet in its dense purple cloud as we chance to step upon it in the path, is familiar to every one. To the mycophagist connoisseur, on the alert for every delectable fungus morsel for his fastidious appetite, the Puff-ball is indeed pleasantly familiar, though a specimen in such a powdery stage as the above is apt to bring only regrets that its discovery has been thus delayed, for in its earlier firm white stage he knows it at his table as a most delicate entrée of "mock omelet."

Puff=ball spore=clouds

The old-time country physician gathered its powdery bag and carefully preserved it for another purpose, its spongy, dusty contents having been a time-honored remedy as a styptic, or for the arrest of hemorrhage from wounds. But by no class of the community perhaps is it so enthusiastically welcomed as by the small boy, to whom it is always a challenge for a kick and a consequent demonstration of smoke worthy of a Fourth-of-July celebration.

A week ago this glistening gray bag, so free with its dust-puff at the slightest touch, was solid in substance and as white as cottage cheese in the fracture. In this condition, sliced and fried, it would have proven a veritable delicacy upon our table, quite suggesting an omelet in consistency and flavor, and in size also, if perchance we had been favored with one of the larger specimens, which frequently approaches the dimensions of a football.

But in a later stage this clear white fracture would have appeared speckled or peppered with gray spots (see page 271), and the next day entirely gray and much softened, and, later again, brown and apparently in a state of decay. But this is not *decay*. This moist brown mass by evaporation becomes powdery, and the Puff-ball is now *ripe*, and preparing for posterity.

Development of spores

Each successive squeeze, as we hold it between our fingers, yields its generous response in a puff of brown smoke, which melts away apparently into air. But the Puff-ball does not thus end in mere smoke. This vanishing purple cloud is composed of tiny atoms, so extremely minute as to require the aid of a powerful microscope to reveal their shapes. Each one of these atoms, so immaterial and buoyant as to be almost without gravity, floating away upon the slightest breath, or even wafted upward by currents of warm air from the heated earth, has within itself the power of reproducing another clump of Puff-balls, if only fortune shall finally lodge it in con-

Buoyant spore=atoms

genial soil. These spores are thus analogous to the seeds of ordinary plants. The number of these vital atoms or spores in a single Puff-ball is almost past computation. Fries, however, an eminent fungologist, went to some pains to estimate this number, and, referring to a certain puff-ball, says: "The spores are infinite. In a single individual of *Reticularia maxima* I have reckoned ten millions so subtle as to resemble thin smoke as light as if raised by evaporation, and dispersed in so many ways—by the sun's attraction, by insects, by adhesion and elasticity—that it is difficult to conceive the spots from which they could be excluded."

Number of spores

We have seen the myriad-fold dispersion of its potential atoms in the cloud of spore-smoke, but who ever thinks of a spore-cloud from a mushroom or a toadstool? Yet the method of the Puff-ball is followed by all the other fungi, with only less conspicuousness. The Puff-ball gives a visible salute, but any one of the common mushrooms or toadstools will afford us a much prettier and more surprising account of itself if we but give it the opportunity. This big yellow toadstool out under the poplar-tree —its golden cap studded with brownish scurfy warts, its under surface beset with closely plaited laminæ or gills — who could ever associate the cloud of dry smoke with this moist, creamy-white surface? We may sit here all day and watch it closely, but we shall see no sign of anything resembling smoke or dust, albeit a filmy emanation is continually eluding us,

Spore-cloud from mushrooms

floating away from beneath its golden cap, the eager breeze taking such jealous care of the continual shower that our eyes fail to perceive a hint of it.

Do you doubt it? You need wait but a few moments for a visible demonstration of the fact in a pretty experiment, which, when once observed, will certainly be resorted to as a frequent pastime in leisure moments when the toadstool or mushroom is available.

Catching the spores

Here is a very ordinary-looking specimen growing beside the stone steps at our back door perhaps. Its top is gray, its gills beneath are fawn-colored. We may shake it as rudely as we will, and yet we shall get no response such as the Puff-ball will give us. But let us lay it upon a piece of white paper, gills downward, on the mantel, and cover it with a tumbler or finger-bowl, so as to absolutely exclude the least admission of air. At the expiration of five minutes, perhaps, we may detect a filmy pinkish-yellow tint on the paper, following beneath the upraised border of the cap, like a shadow faintly lined with white. In a quarter of an hour the tinted deposit is perceptible across the room, and in an hour, if we carefully raise the mushroom, the perfect spore-print is revealed in all its beauty—a spore-tint portrait of the under surface of the mushroom—a pink-brown disk with a white centre, which indicates the point of contact of the cut stem, and white radiating lines, representing the edges of the thin gills, many of them as fine and delicate as a cobweb.

A spore-portrait

Every fresh species experimented with will yield its surprise in the markings and color of the prints.

These spore-deposits are, of course, fugitive, and will easily rub off at the slightest touch. But inas-

MAKING THE PRINT

much as many of these specimens, either from their beauty of form or exquisite color, or for educational or scientific purposes, it will be desirable to preserve, I append simple rules for the making and "fixing" of the prints by a process which was original with the writer, and which he has found most effective for their preservation.

Take a piece of smooth white writing-paper and coat its surface evenly with a thin solution of gum-arabic, dextrine, or other mucilage, and allow it to dry. Pin this, gummed side uppermost, to a board or table, preferably over a soft cloth, so that it will lie perfectly flat. To insure a good print the mushroom specimen should be fresh and firm, and the gills or spore-surface free from breaks or bruises. Cut the stem off about level with the gills, lay the mushroom, spore-surface downward, upon the paper, and cover with a tumbler, finger-bowl, or other vessel with a smooth, even rim, to absolutely exclude the slightest ingress of air. After a few hours, perhaps even less, the spores will be seen through the glass on the paper at the extreme edge of the mushroom, their depth of color indicating the density of the deposit. If we now gently lift the glass, and with the utmost care remove the fungus, perhaps by the aid of pins previously inserted, in a *perfectly vertical* direction, without the slightest side motion, the spore-print in all its beauty is revealed—perhaps a rich brown circular patch with exquisite radiating white lines, marking the direction and edges of the gills, if an Agaric; perhaps a delicate pink, more or less clouded disk, here and there distinctly and finely honey-combed with white lines, indicating that our specimen is one of the polypores, as a Boletus. Other prints will yield rich golden disks, and there will be prints of

Making and fixing spore-prints

Various colors of spores

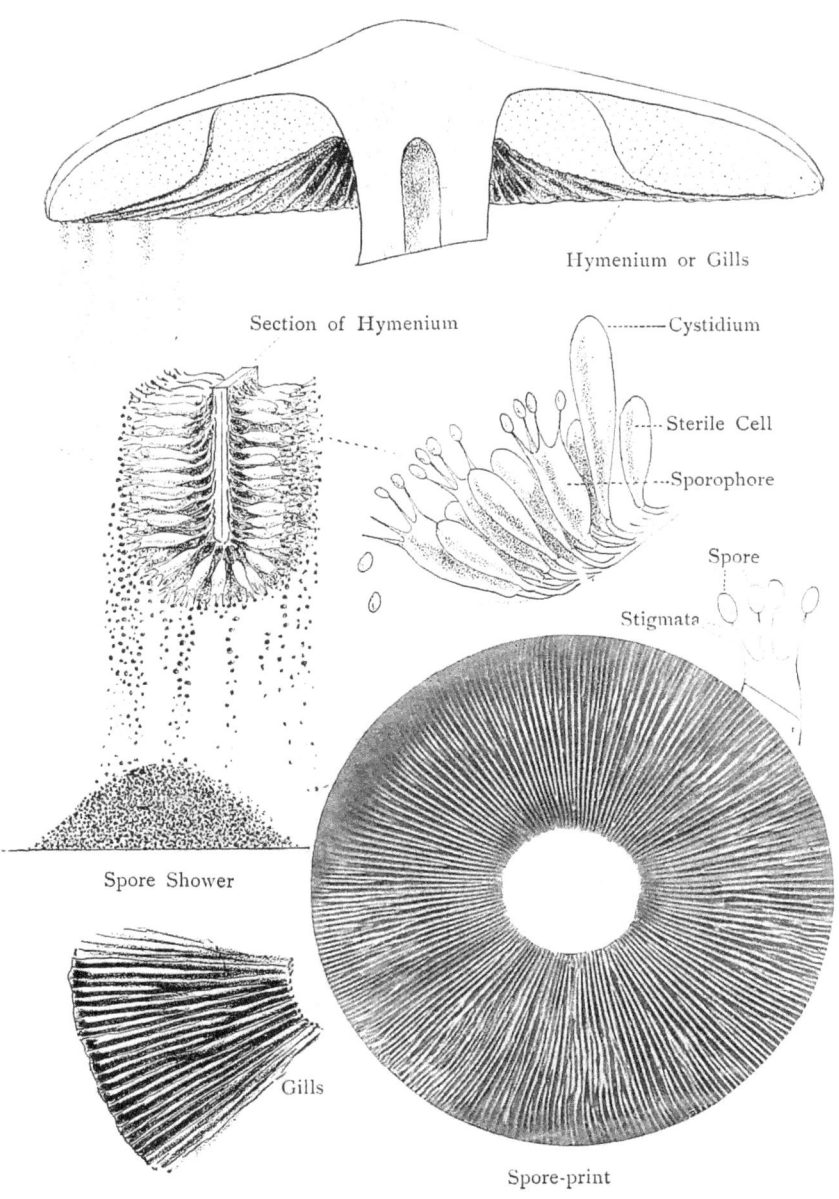

PLATE XXXV.—SPORE-SURFACE OF AN AGARIC

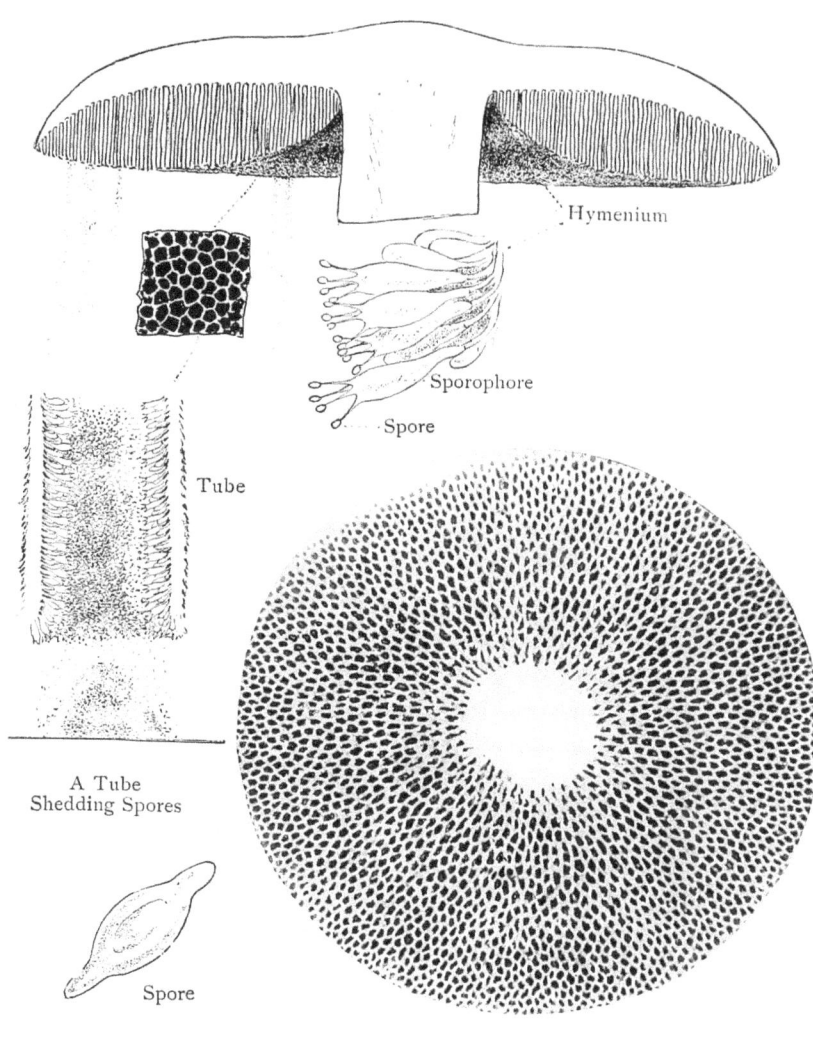

PLATE XXXVI.—SPORE-SURFACE OF POLYPORUS (*BOLETUS*)

varying red, lilac, green, orange, salmon-pink, and brown and purple, variously lined in accordance with the nature of their respective parent gills or pores.

Occasionally we shall look in vain for our print, which may signify that our specimen had already scattered its spores ere we had found it, or, what is more likely, that the spores are *invisi-*

Invisible prints

ble upon the paper, owing to their whiteness, in which case black or colored paper must be substituted for the white ground, when the spores will be beautifully manifest in a white tracery upon the darker background. One of these, from the *Amanita muscarius*, is reproduced in Plate 37. If the specimen is left too long, the spore-deposit is continued upward between the gills, and may reach a quarter of an inch in height, in which case, if extreme care in lifting the cap is used, we observe a very realistic counterfeit of the gills of the mushroom in high relief upon the paper. A print of this kind is of course very fragile, and must be handled with care. But a comparatively slight deposit of the spores, without apparent thickness, will give us the most perfect print, while at the same time yielding the full color. Such a

Fixing the print

print may also be fixed by our present method so as to withstand considerable rough usage, by laying the paper upon a wet towel until the moisture has penetrated through and reached the gum. The spores are thus set, and, upon drying the paper, are securely fixed. Indeed, the moisture exuded by the confined fungus beneath the glass is often sufficient to set the spores.

A number of prints may be obtained successively from a single specimen gathered at its fruitful prime.

To those of my readers interested in the science of this spore-shower I give illustrations of examples of the two more common groups of mushrooms—the Agaric, or gilled mushroom, and the Polyporus, or tube-bearing mushroom. The entire surface of both gills and pores is lined with the spore-bearing membrane or hymenium, the spores being produced in fours from each of the crowded sporophores, and, where all air is absolutely excluded, permitting them to fall directly beneath their point of departure as indicated; in the case of the Agaric, in radiating lines in correspondence with the spaces between the gills; and in Polyporus, directly beneath the opening of each pore, whose inner surface is lined with the sporophores, as shown in Plate 36.

Agarics and Polypores

This dust-shower is continuous in nature after the perfect ripening of the spores, but it is almost impossible to conceive of such an entire absence of moving air under natural conditions as to permit even a visible hint of the spore-shower to appear beneath its respective fungus. An exception to this rule is sometimes to be seen in fungi of massed growth—as, for example, beneath such a cluster as that shown on page 147. Indeed, a correspondent recently described such a cluster as "enveloped in a mist of its own spores floating away in the apparently still air."

Spore=mist from an Agaric

In Plate 38 is shown a spore-print with a peculiar elongated tail. Such was the specimen which I ob-

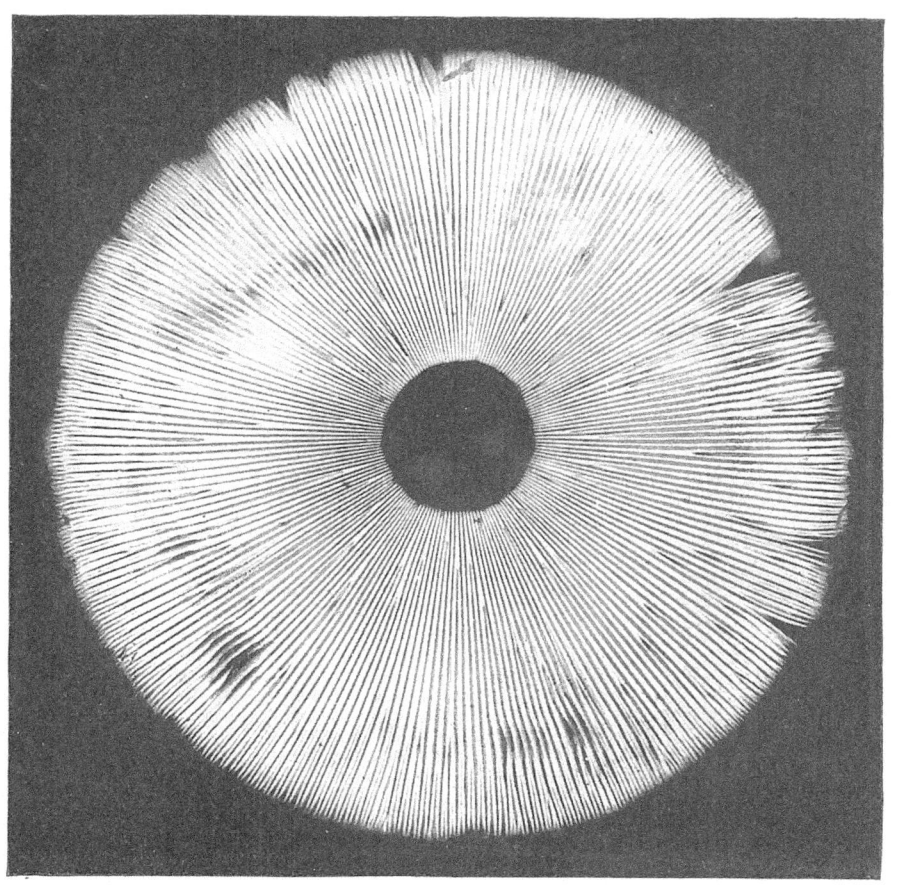

Plate XXXVII.—SPORE-PRINT OF AMANITA MUSCARIUS

PLATE XXXVIII.—ACTION OF SLIGHT DRAUGHT ON SPORES

served when lifting the pasteboard box which had been placed above the mushroom to absolutely exclude the air. The explanation was simple when I discerned that the tapering elongation pointed directly to a tiny hole in the box barely larger than a knitting-needle.

Affected by a pin=hole draft

The greatest portion of the myriads of spores are wafted to the ends of the earth, and form an important element in the so-called "dust" so unwelcome to the tidy housewife. A

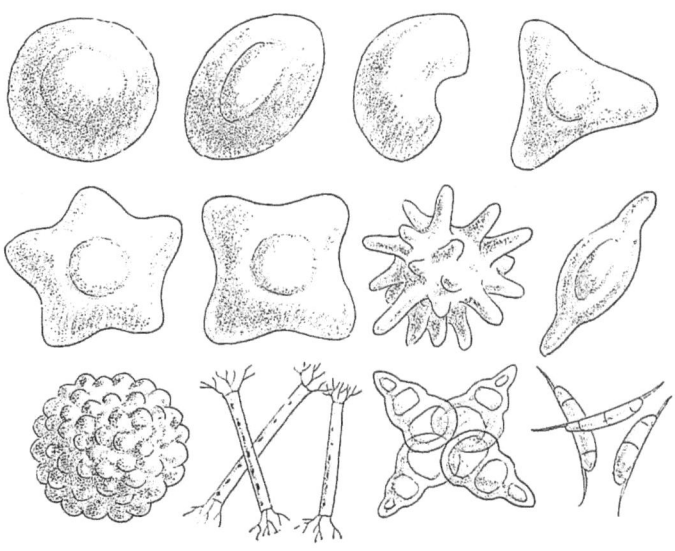

FUNGUS SPORES

sticky glass slide exposed to the deposit of such dust, and placed beneath the microscope, will reveal many fungus spores. The air is full of them.

A few of the various characteristic forms of these fungus-spores is shown on a previous page, somewhat as a powerful microscope would reveal them to us.

But it is only as they chance to alight individually in congenial conditions for growth that they will consent to vegetate. Thus billions of them are doomed to perish without progeny. These whims of habitat among the fungi are almost past belief.

Whims of habitat

Here, for instance, is a tiny Puff-ball hardly larger than the period on this page. It bursts at the summit, and sheds its puff of microscopic spores, so light as to be without gravity, floating and settling everywhere upon the earth, but only as they chance to alight upon the spines of a *dead chestnut-burr* of two years' decay will they find heart to grow. Such is the fastidiousness of the little white mushroom, whose globular caps dot the spines of the decaying chestnut-burrs in so many damp nooks in the woods.

In closing my chapter a glance at the further eccentricities of choice will not be inopportune. I append a few taken at random from the

Curious fastidiousness

pages of Berkeley, which lie open before me. In addition to the general broad distinctions of habitat as "woods," "rotten wood," "old pastures," "dunghills," we find such fastidious selections as the following, each by a distinct species with its own individual whim: "Dead fir-cones, sawdust, beechnuts, plaster walls, old fermenting coffee-grounds, wheat ears, cinders, dead oak leaves, old linen, wheat bread, hoofs, feathers, decayed rope, fat, microscopic lenses, and damp carpets."

A complete list of these exclusive habitats of fungi would well fill a large book, and might indeed almost involve the "index" of our botanies and zoologies, to say nothing of organic substances generally.

Plants, both living and dead, are favorite habitats for various species. The old stems of the common European nettle, according to Cooke, becomes the host of about thirty distinct species of the minute fungi. The toadstool itself is often the victim of other minor species. Insects are a frequent prey. The wasp succumbs to its special fungus parasite, which has formed a home within its body, and the common house-fly is seen in the toils of its similar enemy, as it hangs helpless by its proboscis upon the window-pane, enveloped in the winding-sheet of white mould from the fungus which has done its work within the insect's body. Spiders, locusts, ants, cicadæ, and presumably all insects, are subject to similar fate from their especial parasitic fungi. The fungus thus often comes to the rescue of afflicted humanity in regulating the undue increase of insect pests. Here is a pretty, slender, orange, pointed mushroom growing in the moss. We pluck it from its bed, and it brings to the surface a chrysalis, with the dead moth distinctly seen within the cavity from which its roots spring. When we next come upon this species in the moss, we may confidently predict the discovery of this same species of chrysalis.

A similar long, slender fungus springs from the head of a caterpillar in New Zealand, and at length almost absorbs the insect's body. A similar species upon another caterpillar is carefully collected and desiccated by the Chinese, with whom it forms an important article in their native pharmacopœia, and, moreover, it seems, may be perhaps appropriately included among the "edibles," for are we not assured by these expert and indiscriminate epicures of the chopsticks that this species "makes an excellent dressing for roast duck."

Edible caterpillar fungi

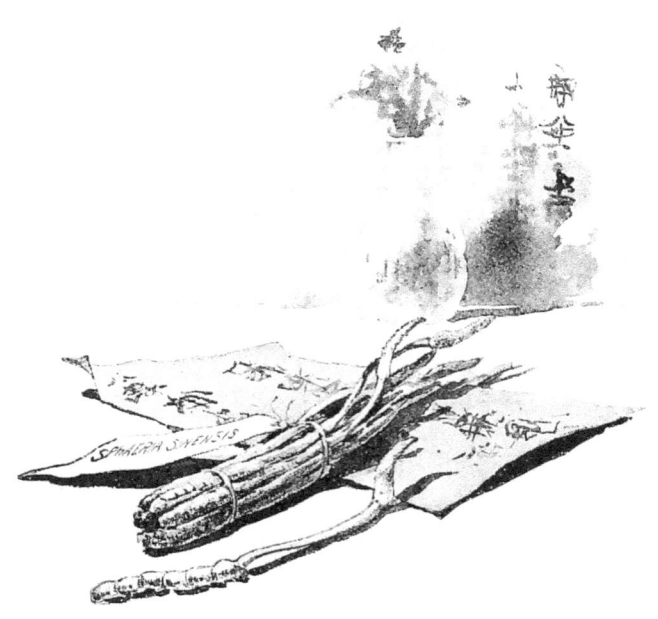

Concerning "Mushromes and Tadstoles"

"AND now for that our fine mouthed and daintie wantons who set such store by their tooth; take so great delight to dress this only dish with their own hands, that they may feed thereon in conceit and cogitation all the while they be handling and preparing the same, furnished in this their businesse with their fine knives and razors of amber and other vessels of silver about them.

"I for my part also am content to frame and accomodate myself to their humourous fancie and will shew unto them in generall certaine observations and rules how to order and use them that they may be eaten with securitie."

Plinius Secundus.

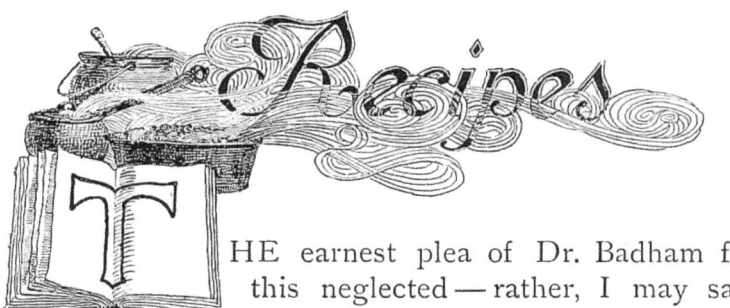

Recipes

THE earnest plea of Dr. Badham for this neglected — rather, I may say, spurned — spontaneous harvest of fungi is well worth emphasizing in our pages; affording, as it does, a most suggestive commentary on the universal popular ignorance, so far as America is concerned, of the economic value of this perennial offering of Nature, which abounds in such luxuriance throughout our continent.

"I have this autumn myself," he writes, "witnessed whole hundred-weights of rich, wholesome diet rotting under trees; woods teeming with food, and not one hand to gather it; and this, perhaps, in the midst of a potato-blight, poverty, and all manner of privations, and public prayers against imminent famine.

The spurned harvest

"I have, indeed, grieved, when I have reflected on the straitened condition of the lower classes this year, to see pounds innumerable of extempore beefsteaks growing on our oaks in the shape of *Fistulina hepatica; Agaricus fusipes*, to pickle, in clusters under them; Puff-balls, which some of our friends have not inaptly compared to sweetbreads for delicacy of their unassisted flavor; Hydna, as good as oysters, which they somewhat resemble in taste; *Agaricus deliciosus*, reminding us of tender lamb kidneys; the beautiful yellow Chantarelle, that *kalon kaigothon* of diet, growing by the bushel, and no basket but our own to pick up a few specimens on our way; the sweet, nutty-flavored Boletus, in vain calling himself '*edulis*' where there was none to believe him; the dainty Orcella; the *Agaricus heterophyllus*, which tastes like a crawfish when grilled; the *Agaricus ruber*, and *Agaricus virescens*, to cook in any way and equally good in all—these are the most conspicuous of the *trouvailles*."

<small>The comprehensive fungus</small>

His remarks applied to Great Britain, and reflected a popular disdain of fungi, which presented a marked contrast to the appreciation of the mushroom of the Continent, where the fungus had become the much-sought *bonne bouche* of the epicure, and the welcome reliance of the peasant poor, to whom it afforded a perfect substitute for the desideratum of animal food commonly denied them by their circumstances.

<small>A reliable crop</small>

This plea of Dr. Badham's is even more pointedly pertinent to the America of the present than it was for his own country at the time; for while, in Great Britain, the mycophagist epicure was even then occasionally to be met with, in America to-day this particular gastronomic specialist is locally conspicuous, or rather notorious, from his very rarity, being popularly

<small>The fungus specialist</small>

considered as a sort of dangerous crank, who should be conservatively muzzled by the authorities, for the safety of himself as well as the public.

In the absence of any adequate popular guide to this great food resource, it may be hoped that this present work may afford not merely an occasional dainty entrée to the menu of the luxurious epicure, but—a far more important consideration—a means of bringing the fungus within reach of the less-favored masses as a never-failing dependence for their daily food.

Mycophagist missionaries

Dr. Badham's further pertinent remarks are worth quoting, in this connection, with emphasis: " As soon as the reader is initiated in this class of dainties he will, I am persuaded, lose no time in making the discovery known to the poor of his neighborhood; while in so doing he will render an important service to the country at large, by instructing the indigent and ignorant in the choice of an ample, wholesome, and excellent article, which they may convert into money or consume at their own tables, when properly prepared, throughout the winter."

Concerning the lavish plenitude of the fungus as a food resource, a passage from a letter of the late Dr. Curtis, of North Carolina, to the Rev. J. M. Berkeley, of England, many years ago, is most significant: " Of this latter quality I had become so well convinced that, during our late war, I sometimes averred—and I doubt if there was much, if any, exaggeration in the assertion — that in some parts of

A suggestive statement

the country I could maintain a regiment of soldiers five months in the year upon mushrooms alone." A statement which doubtless will appear extravagant to those who have been accustomed to consider the one common "mushroom" as the only esculent among the fungi.

As already mentioned previously in my pages, the fungus affords a perfect substitute, chemically and gastronomically, for animal food. The analysis of its substance is almost identical with that of meat, being especially rich in nitrogenous elements, while its flavor and aroma and texture, as served for the table, occasionally so closely imitate that of flesh food as to be actually deceptive. Even in its raw state it would occasionally seem to suggest the same animal similarity. As an illustration, I recall the following striking instance of gastronomic discrimination in a carnivorous appetite, as exemplified in a full-grown pet hawk which I had tethered near my country studio.

Nutritious properties

One day, returning from a toadstool hunt, she observed me approaching with a basketful of mushrooms. They were mostly of the fleshy Boleti species. Supposing that I was bringing her food, she became very demonstrative in her actions, eying me most eagerly, and uttering that peculiar low squeal which seemed to emanate from the region of her appetite. As she approached me, thinking to satisfy her that the basket contained nothing suitable for hawk-food, I tossed her one of the largest of the

A discriminating hawk

mushrooms, which she almost caught in mid-air in her talons. Such was the strength of her clutch that the fungus was scattered in fragments upon the ground, when what was my surprise to observe the bird proceed from one fragment to another in a most ravenous manner, exhibiting all those tactics habitual to the hawk with live prey—the lowering and outspreading of the wings and tail against the ground, the raising of the neck feathers, and the same defiant, defensive mien which she had so often shown on previous occasions when a mouse or a squirrel had been the object of her solicitude. Having eaten the first fungus, I threw her another, which she devoured with the same eagerness, and another, and another, until she had taken five, and her crop was as large as a pint cup; after which she betook herself quietly to her roost on the rail near by, evidently under the supposition that she had broken her fast with a sumptuous meal of rabbit or squirrel flesh.

The *Agaricus ostreatus* is known as the "vegetable oyster"—its flavor in a stew quite closely simulating the flavor of the bivalve; another fungus as the "beefsteak mushroom"—not without good reason; the *Polyporus sulphureus* distinctly suggests the flesh and flavor of chicken; others, as we have seen, resemble kidneys and sweetbread; while the *Agaricus ulmarius* of the elm would seem entitled to its popular name of "fish-mushroom," from the following incident related by Palmer:

Fish, flesh, and fowl

"I recently sent some elm-tree mushrooms to a family where the youngest member is but twenty-one months of age. At breakfast-time she noticed the strange dish, and her father gave her a small piece. ' More fish! more fish!' was the instant response."

Indeed, the vegetarian may humor his humane whim, and still enjoy fish, flesh, and fowl at his table without a qualm of conscience in a menu which, in aroma, quality, and flavor, might well deceive his unconverted omnivorous brother, only at last to win his encomium to the glory of the *multum in parvo* fungus. The possibilities in this direction are suggested in my appended hints for a menu for the vegetarian.

A boon to the vegetarian

In my previous pages I have made occasional reference to the more simple methods of preparation of certain species of fungi for the table, but have reserved extended reference to culinary treatment for the present chapter.

For the benefit of those of my readers who may desire to "humour their delicate fancie" to the full, with the result of a more or less complete disguise of the characteristic mushroom flavor through the arts which are supposed to "assist nature," I append a selected list of favorite recipes for such alleged appetizing sophistication of the mushroom. Many of them will be found equally applicable to other species than that for which they are nominally recommended, especially if such species should possess the same general character as to consistency.

Fungi in the kitchen

The author confesses that he is not in thorough sympathy with the general trend of these ingeniously contrived lures to dyspepsia, whose contemplation may well awaken a sympathetic appreciation of that antique philosophic epigram, "There are as many diseases as cooks"—the discriminating impeachment of Seneca regarding the "*chef à la mode*."

But doubtless the author will be overwhelmingly overruled in his hypercriticisms, and will remain one of a select discriminating minority in continued genuine enjoyment of his *mushrooms*, while the majority of his proselytes to mycophagy will in vain endeavor to detect the mushroom flavor in the obliterating disguise concocted in the kitchen or instigated by the mischievous "receipt-book."

<small>De gustibus non est disputandum</small>

Indeed, the prominence of the spice, clove, nutmeg, thyme, tarragon, and pepper ingredient in most of these "favorite recipes," to say nothing of the champagne, onion, garlic, lemon-juice, cayenne, anchovy, etc., with which the delicately flavored mushrooms are so generally sophisticated in these culinary preparations, would seem to warrant our scepticism as to the value of the epicurean testimony as to the "superior flavor," of the various "Champignons," "Chantarelles," etc., so confidently recommended. The juice of a lemon, or oil of lemon-peel, will absolutely annihilate the peculiar characteristic "fungus" flavor of the average mushroom. The true mushroom epicure, it would seem, should value his *mousseron* not as an absorbent vehicle for the gastronomic conveyance of highly seasoned sauce or dressing, but for the unique individual flavor which differentiates the fungus from other kinds of food.

But we are all allowed to differ in matters of taste, and each must decide for himself or herself what particular disguise is most palatable.

The recipes which follow are from various sources, most of them modifications based upon the earlier epicurean devices of Mrs. Hussey and Dr. Badham, the pioneers of English mycophagy, and of Roques, Persoon, Paulet, Cordier, and other noted European authorities. I am indebted, also, to the works of M. C. Cook, Worthington Smith, W. Robinson, and J. A. Palmer for occasional selections from their recommended recipes.

RECIPES FOR MUSHROOM COOKING

In all cases the mushroom should be fresh, clear and free from the insect indications mentioned on page 131. Some epicures recommend that the specimens be also washed in cold acidulated water and dried in a cloth; for what reason is not clear, unless the mushrooms are sufficiently dirty to require such cleansing process.

1 Mushroom Soup

" Take a good quantity of mushrooms, cut off the earthy ends and wash them; stew them, with some butter, pepper, and salt, in a little good stock until tender; take them out and chop them up until quite small; prepare a good stock as for any other soup, and add it to the mushrooms and the liquor they have been stewed in. Boil all together and serve. If white soup be desired, use the white button-mushrooms and a good veal stock, adding a spoonful of cream or a little milk, as the color may require."—*W. Smith.*

Other mushrooms may be substituted for the ordinary Campestris above mentioned. A very good mock oyster soup may be prepared from the mushrooms Hydnum and the *Agaricus ostreatus.*

2 Purée of Mushrooms

" To make a purée of mushrooms, select such as are of a globular shape, called 'button-mushrooms;' wash them in cold water and wipe them dry; chop them as fine as possible and press them in a cloth; put them in a stewpan with a little butter and pepper; let them stand over a brisk fire, and when the butter is melted squeeze in lemon-juice and add jelly broth, according to the quantity of the mushrooms. Stew until reduced to the consistency of pea-soup, and serve with meat, fish, or poached egg."—*Cooke.*

3 Mushroom Stew

Put about two ounces of butter into a stewpan; when thoroughly melted add a teaspoonful of salt, and from a quarter to half the quantity of black pepper, according to taste, and a small bit of mace or a pinch of powdered nutmeg. Having a pint of the mushrooms in readiness, put them in the pan, cover closely, and stew them till they are tender, which will probably require from twenty minutes to half an hour. The addition of flour stirred in cream or milk, by which the stew is thickened, is by some considered a desirable addition. This recipe is given with special reference to the Campestris, but will be found suitable for other mushrooms of the same consistency.

4 Broiled Mushrooms on Toast

Remove the stems, and place the mushrooms in a double wire broiler over the coals, with the gill sides down, for about two minutes, or even less if the specimens are small. The broiler should then be turned, and the cooking should proceed for two minutes more; towards the end of that time the juicy gills should be sprinkled with salt and pepper, a small piece of butter being finally melted in each as they are served on the hot toast. By this simple method all the natural juices of the mushroom are retained and the true aroma and flavor is conserved. Bacon toasted over the mushrooms is considered by some to improve the flavor.

5 Mushrooms à la Provençal

Take mushrooms of good size, remove the stems and cut their tops in halves or quarters, which, with the chopped stems, should then be immersed in olive oil, spiced with salt, pepper, and a piece of garlic, for about two hours. They should then be put into a stewpan with oil and cooked over a brisk fire. A variation of this method includes the addition of chopped meat and the yolks of two eggs, the whole being slightly browned in the oven before serving.

6 Mushrooms à la Crème

"Trim and rub half a pint of button-mushrooms; dissolve two ounces of butter rolled in flour in a stewpan; then put in the mushrooms, a bunch of parsley, a teaspoonful of salt, half a teaspoonful each of white pepper and powdered sugar; shake the pan around for ten minutes, then beat up the yolks of two eggs with two tablespoonfuls of cream, and add by degrees to the mushrooms. In two or three minutes you can serve them in the sauce."—*Worthington Smith.*

7 Mushroom Ragoût

" Put into a stewpan a little stock, a small quantity of vinegar, parsley and green onions chopped up, salt, and spices. When this is about to boil, the mushrooms being cleaned, put them in. When done remove them from the fire and thicken with yolks of eggs."—*Worthington Smith.* Another recommends that the stew should be poured upon toast, or upon crusts of bread previously fried in butter.

8 Stewed Mushrooms on Toast.

Put a pint of mushrooms into a stewpan, with two ounces of butter rolled in flour, add a teaspoonful of salt, half a teaspoonful of white pepper, a blade of powdered mace, and half a teaspoonful of grated lemon; stew until the butter is all absorbed, then serve on hot toast as soon as the mushrooms are tender.

9 Champignon

" Cut in small pieces and seasoned it makes an excellent addition to stews, hashes, or fried meats; but it should be added only a few minutes before serving, as the aroma is dissipated by over-cooking. It is the mushroom used in the French *à la mode* beef-shops in London."—*Badham*. They may be cooked in any of the methods employed for the ordinary mushroom already noted.

10 Chantarelle Stew

This mushroom, being of rather tough consistency, requires long and slow cooking.

"Cut the mushrooms across and remove the stems; put them into a closely covered saucepan with a little fresh butter, and sweat them until tender at the lowest possible temperature. A great heat always destroys the flavor."—*Mrs. Hussey*.

11 Hydnum Stew

Roques, the French mycologist, says of the *Hydnum repandum*: "The general use of this fungus throughout France, Italy, and Germany leaves no room for doubt as to its good qualities." But very little has been said of its companion species, the *H. caput-medusæ*, described in the foregoing pages, and which is certainly greatly its superior in texture and flavor. Dr. Harkness considers it one of the most delicious morsels among the whole fungus tribe.

Both species, containing naturally less moisture than most mushrooms, are easily dried. When fresh they should be soaked in water and cooked slowly at low temperature and frequently basted, the dried specimens being first soaked in tepid water until their original form and pulpy consistency are nearly regained.

In a purée the Hydnum makes an appetizing dish, with a slight flavor of oysters.

Roques recommends the following recipe for a stew: "Cut the mushrooms into pieces and let them steep in warm water for twenty minutes. Then allow them to simmer for an hour in a pan with butter, pepper, salt, and parsley, with the addition of beef or other gravy."

Mrs. Hussey recommends stewing in brown or white sauce; in the latter case it will closely suggest "oyster sauce."

Another mushroom — the *Lactarius deliciosus* — stewed in a similar manner closely suggests the flavor of lambs' kidneys.

12 Roast Mushrooms

Mr. Palmer recommends the following: "Cut the larger specimens into fine pieces and place them in a small dish, with salt, butter, and pepper to taste; put in about two tablespoonfuls of water, then fill the dish with the half-open specimens and the buttons; cover tightly and place in the oven, which must not be overheated, for about ten minutes. The juice of the larger mushrooms will keep them moist, and, if fresh, yield a most abundant gravy."

13 Baked Russula

See that the mushrooms are free from dirt and grit on tops and stems, or rinse in cold water, afterwards wiping them dry and shaking off the water from the gills; make a mince of the stems, bread-crumbs, sweet herbs, pepper, salt, and a little butter or oil; pile this upon the gills; place the mushrooms in a shallow dish in a hot oven and baste them frequently with the melted butter or oil. In about fifteen minutes they will be ready to serve.

The Oyster Mushroom or its congener, the *Agaricus ulmarius*, might both be treated by this method, the oyster or fish-like flavor of these species thus affording a distinct second course for our menu. Either of these Pleurotus species may also be treated so as to closely suggest an escalop of oyster or fish.

14 Baked Procerus

Remove the stems; do not rinse the mushrooms unless they are soiled, and this species is usually conspicuously clean; put some slices of toast in a well-buttered pie-dish, and, with a little melted butter or cream poured over them, lay in the mushrooms; sprinkle with pepper, salt, and a small quantity of minced parsley which has previously been rubbed with onion or garlic; cover the dish with a plate and bake in a hot oven for fifteen minutes and serve in the dish. The aroma is thus conserved, and, upon being released at the table, will prove a most savory appetizer.

15 Cottagers' Procerus Pie

The following appetizing recipe is recommended by Robinson: "Cut fresh Agarics in small pieces, cover the bottom of a pie-dish with small, thin slices of bacon, and place the mushroom fragments upon them, with the addition of salt and pepper; upon this place a layer of mashed potatoes, following again with other similar layers of bacon, mushrooms, and potatoes, until the dish is filled, the last layer of potato answering for a crust; bake in the oven for half an hour, and brown before a brisk fire."

Doubtless many other species of mushroom would lend themselves equally well to this particular treatment.

16 Baked Gambosus

" Place some fresh-made toast, nicely divided, on a dish, and put the Agarics upon it; pepper, salt, and put a small piece of butter on each; then pour on each one a tablespoonful of milk or cream, and add a single clove to the whole dish; place a bell-glass or inverted basin over the whole; bake twenty minutes, and serve up without removing the glass until it comes to the table, so as to preserve the heat and aroma, which, on lifting the cover, will be diffused through the room."—*Cooke*. "A great quantity of gravy comes out of it, mingled, in the case of a good specimen, with osmazome, which tastes very much like the similar brown exudation on the surface of a roast leg of mutton."—*Robinson*.

17 Fried Mushrooms on Toast

Place a pint of mushrooms in a pan, with a piece of butter about the size of an egg; sprinkle in a teaspoonful of salt, and half a teaspoonful of pepper; when the butter is nearly absorbed, thicken with fresh butter and flour and pour upon hot toast, which should be served hot.

18 Mushrooms with Bacon

Fry a few rashers of nice streaky bacon in the pan in the usual manner; when nearly done add a dozen or so of mushrooms, and fry them slowly until they are cooked. In this process they will absorb all the fat of the bacon, and, with the addition of a little salt and pepper, will form a most appetizing breakfast relish.

19 Mushrooms en Caisse

The following is recommended as a dainty by Worthington Smith: "Peel the mushrooms lightly and cut them into pieces; put them into cases of buttered paper, with a bit of butter, parsley, green onions, and shallots chopped up; salt and pepper; dress them on a gridiron over a gentle fire and serve in the cases." The cases might be made of pastry.

20 Hungarian Soup of Boleti

" Dry the Boleti in the oven; soak the mushrooms in tepid water, thickening with toasted bread till the whole be of the consistency of a purée; then rub through a sieve, throw in some stewed boleti, boil together, and serve with the usual condiments."— *Paulet.*

21 Boletus Fritters

Persoon recommends this method of treatment of the Boletus as very appetizing: The fritters may be prepared in the method ordinarily adopted, the slices of the mushroom being dipped in batter and browned either in the frying-pan or in the hot fat, after the manner of the doughnut.

22 Beefsteak Mushroom

This species is claimed to resemble meat in flavor

more than any other fungus. The gravy, in quality and color, would certainly deceive a most discriminating palate. Like many of the Polyporei, it is comparatively slow in maturing, occasionally, it is said, requiring two weeks ere it reaches its prime, when it may acquire a large size.

It should be gathered before its maturity to insure tenderness, though the older, tougher individuals, cut in pieces and cooked separately, will yield a quantity of rich red gravy, to be added to the dish of more tender specimens. "If it is not beef itself," says Mrs. Hussey, "it is sauce for it." "If sliced and grilled it would pass for a good beefsteak," says Cooke, with truth. Mrs. Hussey recommends that it should be sliced and macerated in salt, the deep-red liquor which exudes should be put hot into a dish with a little lemon-juice and minced shallots, and a broiled steak deposited in it. It may also be variously stewed or fricasseed with excellent results, and affords a delicious soup with savor closely suggesting beef broth or *consommé clair*. A "beef-steak" pie made on the foregoing recipe prescribed for the Procerus would doubtless prove a most appetizing entrée.

23 The Oyster Mushroom

"It may be cooked in any way that an oyster is, and is equally good in all," says a distinguished connoisseur—in soups, stewed, broiled, curried, baked, in the form of an escalop, patties, or *vol-au-vent*, or fried with butter in the form of fritters. In all cases where the fungus itself is to be eaten, the specimens should be young and tender, the older individuals, if free from insects, might be used for soups. See Recipe 13.

24 Polyporus Stew

The beautiful sulphur-colored Polyporus described in my previous pages when stewed closely suggests the tender white meat of chicken or veal, and might lend itself to various deceptive dishes, as, for instance, soups, croquettes, fricassees, or patties.

Only the tender young plant should be employed, and a little experience will suggest various appetizing methods of treatment.

25 Ragoût of Morels or Helvella

The following is an old-time recipe of Persoon: "Pick and clean your fungi and cut them in two; wash and dry them well by wiping; then put them in a stewpan with butter, or a piece of ham or bacon; place them over a brisk fire, and when the butter is melted squeeze in a little lemon-juice, give a few turns, and then add salt, pepper, and a little grated nutmeg; cook slowly for an hour, pouring on at intervals small quantities of beef gravy or jelly broth to prevent burning; when done, thicken with yolks of eggs." The lemon-juice is omitted by many, who consider it a positively unpalatable as well as unwholesome ingredient.

26 Stuffed Morels

Dr. Badham's work contains the following recipes from Persoon, which, from the peculiar construction of the fungus, affords a contrast to ordinary methods: "Choose the freshest and whitest Morels; open the stalk at the bottom; wash and wipe them well; fill with veal stuffing, anchovy, or any rich *farce* you choose, securing the ends and dressing between slices of bacon. Serve with a sauce."

27 Morelles à la Italienne

Here is another skilful compound from the same source: "Having washed and dried the mushrooms, divide them across; put them on the fire with some parsley, scallion, chervil, burnet, tarragon, cives, a little salt, and two spoonfuls of fine oil; stew until the juice runs out, then thicken with a little flour. Serve with bread-crumbs and a squeeze of lemon."

28 Clavaria Stew

Badham gives the following recipe for the Clavaria, or coral fungus: "After sousing in tepid water and wiping perfectly clean, the fungus should be 'sweated' over a slow fire, afterwards to be strained and the liquor thrown away; stew for an hour; add salt, pepper, cloves, and parsley to taste, masking with plain stock and dredging occasionally with flour. Thicken with yolks of eggs and cream."

29 Fried Clavaria

The simple process of browning in butter or oil in the frying-pan, with the addition of pepper and salt, and serving hot on buttered toast or with fried eggs, will be found a most palatable method of treating this fungus. For those who are willing to sacrifice the characteristic *fungus* flavor to a savor more pronounced, the Clavaria is also said to be delicious when fried with onions or with curry in the usual method.

30 Puff=ball
Fritters, Omelettes, Sweetbreads, and Soufflé

As already described, the Puff-balls in their white-pulp condition are esculent and afford a delicate relish. The species Giganteus sometimes attains a diameter of nearly two feet, and where such a specimen or even much smaller ones are situated at an easily available distance, we may profit by the hint of Vitadini, the Italian mycologist: "Cut off a slice at a time, cutting it horizontally, and using great care not to disturb its growth, to prevent decay, and thus one may have a fritter every day for a week." Dr. Curtis calls this species the "Southdown of mushrooms." His opinion of its merits as food will be shared by others who give it a trial: "It has a delicacy of flavor that makes it superior to any omelette I have ever eaten. It seems, furthermore, to be so digestible as to adapt itself to the most delicate stomach." Mrs. Hussey, the pioneer English authority, recommends the following recipe: "First remove the outer skin; cut in slices half an inch thick; have ready some chopped herbs, pepper, and salt; dip the slices in the yolk of egg, and sprinkle the herbs upon them; fry in fresh butter and eat immediately."

The extreme tenderness and delicacy of the Puff-ball thus cooked resembles a soufflé, and suggests many possibilities of appetizing variations and combinations, as, for example, with jelly, in the form of an entremet or dessert. By many the flavor of the Puff-ball has been compared to "sweetbread," and doubtless so cooked and served would afford an agreeable variation in the menu. Indeed, it may be prepared in a variety of ways, as suggested for other species, but from its peculiar consistency is particularly adapted to frying in the pan. With chopped ham or thinly sliced smoked beef it might furnish a good substitute for the ham-omelette or frizzled beef.

Another addition to our entremets might be availed of in the "jelly mushroom," Hydnum, or *Tremelodon gelatinosum*, which is not described in this volume. It is eaten raw, either plain or with milk and sugar, and is said to be of most delicate flavor.

31 Mushroom Salad

According to Cooke, the Beefsteak mushroom before mentioned is employed as an entremet in Vienna, the fresh fungus being cut in thin slices and eaten as a salad. The fresh, crisp young Russula mushrooms thus served also furnish a very appetizing relish, with the usual varieties of dressing as in the various sauces, mayonnaise, French dressing, etc. The *Polyporus sulphureus* having been boiled and allowed to cool might furnish a deceptive "chicken" salad. Doubtless other species of mushrooms—Clavaria, for example—would lend themselves acceptably to this method of serving. Cordier recommends this latter species as "appetizing even when raw."

32 Pickled Mushrooms

Select the mushrooms in the round-button condition and before expansion; immerse them in cold water for a few moments, then drain them; cut off the stalks, and gently rub off the outer skin with a moist flannel dipped in salt; boil the vinegar, adding to each quart two ounces of salt, half a nutmeg grated, a dram of mace, and an ounce of white pepper-corns; put the mushrooms into the vinegar for ten minutes over the fire; then pour the whole into small jars, taking care that the spices are equally divided; let them stand a day, then cover them.

33 Mushroom Catsup

Large quantities of mushrooms of various species are annually consumed in Europe in the manufacture of catsup. Following is one of the many favorite foreign recipes:

Place the Agarics, of as large a size as you can procure, layer by layer in a deep pan; sprinkle each layer with a little salt; the next day stir them well several times, so as to mash and extract their juice; on the third day strain off the liquor, measure and boil for ten minutes, and then to every pint of liquor add half an ounce of black pepper, a quarter of an ounce of bruised ginger-root, a blade of mace, a clove or two, and a teaspoonful of mustard-seed; boil again for half an hour, put in two or three bay-leaves, and set aside until quite cold; pass through a strainer, and bottle; cork well and dip the ends of the bottle in melted resin or beeswax; a very little Chili vinegar is an improvement, and some add a glass of port-wine or of ale to every bottle. Care should be taken that the spice is not so abundant as to overpower the true flavor of the mushrooms.

34 Dried Mushrooms

It will often happen in a normal fungus season that the production will exceed the possibility of consumption, and thousands of pounds of delicious mushrooms will thus be left to decay in their haunts.

The process of drying mushrooms for winter use is in most extensive practice by the peasantry of Europe and Britain, who thus find an all-the-year-round dependence upon mushroom diet.

With most species this process of desiccation is so simple that it is recommended, in the confident belief that, once tried, the winter mushroom will hereafter afford a frequent relish upon many a board and will well repay the slight trouble in their summer preparation.

In most of the Agarics—notably the Campestris, Procerus, Champignon, Russula, Chantarelle—simply threading on strings and hanging in the sun and wind, or festooned above the kitchen range, will be sufficient to reduce them to complete dryness in a few hours. Indeed, some of these, such as the Procerus and Champignon, dry spontaneously in their haunts, and may be thus gathered.

In the instances of more fleshy fungi, such as the Boleti, Polyporei, and Coprinus, more rapid desiccation is necessary. By exposing them in the sun on a tin roof or absorbent paper the moisture is rapidly evaporated. They might also be suspended above the kitchen range in a wire basket and thus quickly dried. In Boleti the drying is facilitated by the removal of the whole pore layer, which is easily separated from the cap.

The Clavaria and Morel are very simply dried, even in ordinary house temperature. Strung upon threads and suspended in the sun or near the fire they would very quickly be reduced to absolute dryness.

Mushrooms thus treated seem to retain their aroma; in Procerus, Clavaria, Morel, Helvella, and "Fairy-ring" being intensified above that of their moist condition and most appetizing.

The desiccated specimens should be kept in a dry place, with good circulation of air, or enclosed in hermetically sealed tin boxes; in the latter case being occasionally examined to insure against mould by possible absorption of moisture.

When desired for use they are simply soaked in tepid water, which, by gradual absorption, causes the specimens occasionally to assume almost their original dimensions and juicy character, when they should be treated as recommended for the fresh mushrooms.

For the benefit of the vegetarian, or the curiously or experimentally inclined, I append a few suggestions apropos of a *menu à la mode*, in which the fungus might be employed with good effect as a rival to the familiar established prandial delights. Each selection is numbered with reference to its particular descriptive or suggestive paragraph in the preceding pages of the chapter.

A feast based upon these recommendations, re-enforced with appropriate adjuncts — the "mother"-born vinegar, the fungus-leavened loaf, the fungus-foaming beaker — might cumulatively prove a persuasive plea for the creed of vegetarianism.

Menu

Potages

Consommé de bœuf clair, 22
Potage à la purée d'huîtres, 1, 11, 13
Potage à la purée de bœuf, 22
Potage à la purée de volaille, 24

Poissons

Côtelettes de poisson—Sauce aux champignons, 13
Escalope de poisson, 13

Hors-d'oeuvres

Croquettes de ris de veau, 24
Bouchées au poulet, 24

Relevée

Filet de bœuf aux champignons, 22, 23

Entrées

Omelette aux jambon, 30
Rognons d'agneau, 11
Paté de biftecks, 22
Beignettes d'huîtres, 13, 23
Huîtres en curry, 23
Petits vols-au-vent d'huîtres ou bouchées d'huîtres, 13, 23
Fricassée de poulet, 24

Entremets

Salad de Russula au mayonnaise, 31
Salad de Fistulina, 31
Salad de Clavaria, 31
Salad de volaille, 31

Dessert

Omelette soufflé au gelée, 30
Pouding soufflé, 30
Gelée de Hydnum, 30

Bibliography

AMERICAN

1. *Geological and Natural History Survey of North Carolina.* Part III. Botany. Containing a catalogue of the indigenous and naturalized plants of the State. By Rev. M. A. Curtis, D.D., etc. Raleigh, 1867. (Out of print.)

2. *Mushrooms of America.* Edible and Poisonous. Edited by Julius A. Palmer, Jr. Numerous colored plates. Published by L. Prang & Co., Boston, 1885.

3. *About Mushrooms.* A Guide to the Study of Esculent and Poisonous Fungi. A collection of various articles upon the subject. By Julius A. Palmer. Lee & Shepard, Boston, 1894.

4. *Boleti of the United States.* A catalogue containing full descriptions of one hundred and eight species. (No illustrations.) By Professor Charles H. Peck, State Botanist, State Hall, Albany, N. Y. Annual Report of the State Botanist issued by the Board of Regents, Albany University.

Professor Peck has also published a series of papers on "Edible Mushrooms" in *The Country Gentleman,* of Albany, N. Y. A new work from him on this subject is in preparation.

5. *Pacific Coast Fungi.* By Dr. H. W. Harkness and Justin P. Moore. 1880. A catalogue.

6. *The Deadly and Minor Poisons of Mushrooms.* By Charles McIlvaine. Reprint from the *Therapeutic Gazette.* George S. Davis, Detroit, Mich. Quoted in present volume. Captain McIlvaine is also the author of several popular articles on the subject of esculent mushrooms which have appeared in various journals and magazines.

7. *Fungi Caroliniani Exsiccati.* Five Fasciculi, one hundred specimens in each. By H. W. Ravenel, of Aiken, S. C. John Russell, Charleston.

8. *Bulletins of United States Department of Agriculture, Washington, D. C.* By Thomas M. Taylor, Chief of the Division of Microscopy. Washington, D. C., 1893–94. Five issues, with many colored plates of various specimens, both edible and poisonous; also full directions for cultivation of the common mushroom.

9. *Notes for Mushroom Eaters.* By W. G. Farlow. Pamphlet. Illustrated. Garden & Forest Publishing Co., New York.

ENGLISH

10. *Illustrations of British Mycology.* (Hand-painted.) By Mrs. T. J. Hussey. Reeve Brothers, London, 1847. An admirable work, the pioneer treatise in Great Britain; rare; reference copies only in prominent libraries.

11. *Esculent Funguses of England.* By Rev. Dr. C. D. Badham. With twenty colored plates. 8vo. L. Reeve & Co., London. 1870.

12. *A Plain and Easy Account of the British Fungi;* with Descriptions of the Esculent and Poisonous Species, Details of the Principles of Scientific Classification, and a Tabular Arrangement of Orders and Genera. By M. C. Cooke, M.A., LL.D. With twenty-four colored plates. R. Hardwick, Piccadilly, London, 1871. An excellent, inexpensive, and popular hand-book.

13. *Outlines of British Fungology.* Containing Characters of above a Thousand Species of Fungi, and a Complete List of all that have been described as Natives of the British Isles. By Rev. M. J. Berkeley, M.A., F.L.S. Lovell Reeve, Henrietta Street, Covent Garden, London, 1860. Beautifully illustrated with twenty-four lithographic hand-colored plates by W. Fitch, each plate presenting several species, and including a number of the esculent.

14. *Mushrooms and Toadstools:* How to Distinguish Easily the Differences between Edible and Poisonous Fungi. With two large sheets containing figures of twenty-nine edible and thirty-one poisonous species drawn the natural size, and colored from living specimens. By Worthington T. Smith, F.L.S. 2d edition, R. Hardwick, 192 Piccadilly, London, 1875.

15. *A Selection of the Eatable Funguses of Great Britain.* Edited by Robert Hogg, LL.D., and Geo. W. Johnson, F.R.H.S. Numerous excellent hand-colored plates.

16. *Fungi: Their Nature and Uses.* By M. C. Cooke, M.A., LL.D.; edited by the Rev. M. J. Berkeley, M.A., F.L.S. In "International Scientific Series." D. Appleton & Co., N. Y. A very full and condensed epitome of the science of fungology.

17. *Hand-book of British Fungi.* By M. C. Cooke. 2 vols. Macmillan & Co., London, 1871.

18. *Illustrations of British Fungi.* Atlas to accompany above. By M. C. Cooke. Williams & Norgate, London, 1889.

19. *Scottish Cryptogamic Flora.* 6 vols. By R. R. Greville, 1823.

20. *Fungi-hunters' Guide.* By William D. Hay. Swan Sonnenschein, Lowrey & Co., London, 1887.

21. *Elementary Text-book.* By William D. Hay. Swan Sonnenschein, Lowrey & Co., London, 1887.

22. *British Fungi.* By John Stevenson. William Blackwood & Sons, London, 1886.

23. *Mushroom Culture.* By W. Robinson. F. Warne & Co., London, 1870. Containing full directions for the cultivation of mushrooms; also an extended chapter upon common wild species. Illustrated with wood-cuts, numerous recipes, etc.

FRENCH

24. *Plantes Usuelles.* Par Joseph Roches. Vol. IV., containing the Edible and Poisonous Fungi: also his Histoire des Champignons Comestibles et Téné-neux. Elegantly illustrated. Paris, 1838.

25. *Les Champignons:* Histoire, Description, Culture, Usages des Espèces Comestibles, Vénéneuses, Suspectes, etc. Par F. S. Cordier. With sixty chromo-lithographs. 4th edition. Paris, 1876.

26. *Histoire Naturelle des Champignons.* By G. Sicard. C. H. Delagrave, Paris, 1883. Numerous colored plates. Rare. Copy in Astor Library, N. Y.

27. *Botanique Cryptogamique, ou Histoire des Familles Naturelles des Plantes Inférieures.* Par J. Payer, Docteur ès Sciences, etc. With 1105 engravings on wood. Victor Masson, Paris, 1850.

28. *Des Champignons.* (Orfila Prize Essay.) By Emile Boudier. J. B. Ballière, Paris, 1866.

29. *Champignons.* By L. M. Gautier. J. B. Ballière et Fils. Paris, 1884.

30. *Figures Peintes de Champignons.* By Captain L. Lucand. Friedlander & Son, Berlin, 1882. (Reference copy at Massachusetts Horticultural Society.)

31. *Les Champignons.* By J. Moyen. J. Rothschild, Paris, 1889.

32. *Nouvelle Flore.* By J. Constantin and Leon Dufour. Paul Dupont, Paris, 1891.

ACKNOWLEDGMENTS, 40.
Agaricaceæ, order of the, 77.
Agaricini, 75-178; botanical characters of, 79.
Agarics, edible, 80-178; Curtis's list of, 9-12.
Agaricus, 43, 44; vegetation of, 44-47, 85-92, 107; botanical characters of, 77-79, 283.
Agaricus, species of :—*Amanita*, see Amanita ;—*arvensis*, 85, 91; epicurean opinions of, 94 ;—*campestris*, 9, 13, 21, 24, 80-95, 307, 308, 321; the "Mushroom," 16-22; variations in, 89-93; spore-print of, 283 ;—*candicans*, 86 ;—*euosmus*, 147 ;—*fusipes*, 299 ;—*gambosus*, 95-101; to cook, 313;—*heterophylla*, see Russula ;—*Marasmius oreades*, 101-108; —*melleus*, 10, 28 ;—*orcella*, 300 ;—*ostreatus*, 10, 26, 141-148, 303, 307 ;—*pratensis*, 91 ;—*procerus*, 10, 86, 87, 113-119, 312, 321;—*ruber*, 300 ;—*ulmarius*, 10, 26, 27, 148-154, 303, 312;—*vaporarius*, 91;—*villaticus*,91; —*virescens*, 300. See, also, Russula, Coprinus, Lactarius, Chantarelle, and Marasmius.
Agrippina, victim of Amanita, 59.
Amanita, genus of, readily identified, 2, 23, 74, 273.
— Botanical characters of, 29, 33, 41-51, 79, 273.
— The cup or volva in, 29, 33, 47, 48, 57, 74, 273.
— Vegetation and development of, 44, 45, 74; the veil or shroud of, 48.
— Fatalities from eating, 2, 15, 29, 60; a dangerous enemy, 15, 23, 29; "silver test" upon, 26; effect of salt and heat upon, 29.
— Poison of, 48, 60; chemical nature of poison of, 48, 61; Czar Alexis, 52; Agrippina, 59; intoxication from, 59, 60; dipsomaniacs, 59, 60; isolation of poison of, 61; absorption of poison of, by contact and odor, 30, 69; diagnosis and treatment of poison of,

38, 39; antidote for poison of, 61–68 ; report of a case of poisoning by, 63–66 ; poison of, extracted by vinegar, 71.

Amanita, Poisonous species of :—*vernus*, 17, 25, 51 ;—*muscarius*, 51, 73 ; spore-print of, 289, 291;—*phalloides*, 51, 74.

— Edible species of, 73 ; *Cæsarea*, *rubescens*, *strobiliformis*, 9, 12, 48.

Amanitine, 60 ; antidote, 62.

Alexis, Czar, victim of Amanita, 52.

America and Europe, comparative appreciation of fungi in, 299.

American and European fungi identical, 12.

American mycophagists, 8, 9, 15.

Antidotes for mushroom poisoning, 62, 67, 68.

Ants attacked by fungi, 295.

Asci in fungi, 256.

Ascomycetes, 256.

Asiatic Russia, Amanita dipsomaniacs of, 59.

BACTERIUM bacillus, 7, 8.

Badham, Dr. C. D., quoted, xii., 12, 13, 40, 177, 189, 237, 246, 299, 301, 306, 310, 316. Bibliography, No. 11, 326.

Baked mushrooms, 311–313.

Basket for gathering mushrooms, 36.

"Beefsteak" mushroom, 11, 27, 213–217, 303 ; to cook, 314 ; as salad, 319.

Bees and wasps, 36.

Beetles infesting fungi, 37.

Belladonna. See Atropine.

Berkeley, Rev. M. J., variations in Campestris, 40, 91 ; quoted, 107, 237, 246, 294, 301. Bibliography, Nos. 13 and 16, 326.

Bibliography — American, 325 ; English, 326 ; French, 327.

Bitter Boletus, 208.

Blights, 7.

Blue mould, 78.

Blue-stain Boleti, 196.

Boleti, 182–213 ; botanical characters of, 181–184, 285 ; hawk fed upon, 302 ; fritters of, 314 ; soup of, 314 ; to dry, 321.

Boletus, characters of, 182 ; various edible, 10, 26, 182–213 ; spore-print of, 285.

Boletus,—alveolatus, 183, 201, 208 ;— *castaneus*, 10 ; —*chrysenteron*, 195–201 ; — *collinitus*, 10 ; — *cyanescens*, 201, 207 ; cone-like, 202 ;—*edulis*, 10, 13, 16, 18, 189, 190, 300 ; artificial cultivation of, 86 ; crimson, 213 ; —*elegans*, 10 ;—*felleus*, 207, 208–213 ; — *flavidus*, 10 ;—*granulatus*, 10 ;— *luteus*, 10 ;—*satanas*, 207, 208 ;— *scaber*, 10, 191–195 ;—*subtomentosus*, 10, 26, 183, 195 ; blue stain of, 196, 201, 207 ;—*strobilomyces*, 202–207 ; spore-print of, 281 ;—*versipellis*, 10.

Botanical discrimination, 31, 32.

— discrimination of Amanita. See Amanita.

Boudier, Emile. Bibliography, No. 28, 327.

Bovista nigrescens, 10.

— *plumbea*, 10.

Broiled mushrooms, 308.

Bubbola maggiore. See Pasture Mushroom.

Bulbosine, 60.

CAMPESTRIS. See Agaricus.

Cantharellus,—cibarius, 10, 27, 172–178, 300 ; — *aurantiacus*, 178 ; to cook, 310 ; drying of, 321.

Caterpillar fungi, 295.

Catsup, Mushroom, 320.

Champignon "Fairy-Ring," 27, 87, 95 ; to cook, 309 ; dried, 321.

— Poisonous, 108, 113.

Chantarelle. See Cantharellus.

"Chef à la mode," the, 305.

Chemical analysis of fungi, 14, 302.

INDEX

Chestnut-burr fungus, 294.
Chestnut tongue. See Fistulina.
Chicken flavor in mushrooms, 303, 316.
Chinese caterpillar fungus, 296.
Cicada fungus, 295.
Classification of fungi, 77, 78.
Claudius, Emperor, poisoned, 59.
Clavariei, 231, 247–256.
Clavaria, Various, 10, 11 ;—*amethystina, fastigiata, flava, rugosa, stricta, umbrina*, 255 ;—*botrytis*, 256 ;—*formosa*, 247; to cook, 317 ; used as salad, 319 ; to dry, 322.
Club fungi. See Clavaria.
Cogomelos. See Pasture Mushroom.
Colored plates of the book, 39.
Coniomycetes, 78.
Consommé from mushrooms, 315.
Cooke, Rev. Dr. M. C., 40, 59, 214, 237, 273, 295, 306, 307, 313, 315. Bibliography, Nos. 12, 16, 17, 326 ; No. 18, 327.
Cooking fungi, 72, 306–322.
Coprinus, 87; to dry, 321 ;—*atramentarius*, 11, 27, 28, 161, 163 ;—*comatus*, 11, 87, 154–160.
Coral fungi. See Clavaria.
Cordier, F. S., 246, 248, 306, 319. Bibliography, No. 25, 327.
Correspondents, 2–6.
Cortinarius castaneus, cinnamomeus, violaceus, 11.
Cosmopolitan fungi, 12.
Coulemelle. See Pasture Mushroom.
Crimson Boletus, 213.
Cryptogamia, the, 7.
Crystals on drying fungi, 227.
Culinary "treatment" of fungi, 72, 214, 304.
Cultivation of mushrooms, 85, 86. Bibliography, No. 8, 325 ; No. 23, 327.
"Cup," the, in Amanita, 29, 33, 47, 48, 57, 74, 273.
Currie, Dr., on Amanita poison, 60.
Curtis, Rev. M. A., pioneer American mycophagist, 9, 32, 40.

Curtis's, Rev. M. A., list of edible mushrooms, 9–12 ; quoted, 219, 245, 301, 318. Bibliography, No. 1, 325.
Cystidium, the, 77, 256.

DEADLY mushrooms and toadstools, 2, 3, 43–74.
Deaths by fungi, 43, 61.
Decaying fungi, 6, 25, 30, 278.
Delagrave, C. H. Bibliography, No. 26, 327.
Desiccation of fungi, 107, 119, 246, 262, 321.
Diagnosis and treatment of mushroom poisoning, 38, 63–68.
Doe-skin mushroom. See *Hydnum repandum*.
Dried fungi. See Desiccation of fungi.
Dufour, J. Constantin and Leon. Bibliography, No. 32, 327.
Dust-like fungi, 78.

ECONOMIC fungology, 7, 13, 14.
Edible Amanitæ, 9, 12, 73.
Edible mushrooms, number of species, 2, 7, 32, 60; list of, by Curtis, 9–12; popular tests for identification, 22, 23; become poisonous from contact with Amanita, 70.
Elm mushroom, 10, 26, 27, 148–154, 303, 312.
Elvellacei, 231. See Helvella.
Emetic mushroom. See Russula.
Epicurean perversity, 72.
European and American fungi identical, 12.
European mycologists, 14, 326, 327.

FAIRY-RING mushroom, 95, 101–108 ; cause of "ring," 102, 107 ; recipes for cooking, 107, 108; false or poisonous, 108, 113.
False Champignon, 108.
Farlow, W. G. Bibliography, No. 9, 326.
"Fish mushroom," 154, 303, 312.

Fistulina hepatica, 11, 26, 27, 213, 299, 303; to cook, 314; as salad, 319.
Fly, Fungus attacking, 295.
Fly-poison, Amanita, 27, 51, 52, 72. See *Amanita muscarius.*
Food, Fungi as, 8, 13–15, 35, 221, 245, 299–323.
"Foxfire," 227.
France, Fungus-eaters of, 14.
Fried mushrooms, 313–318.
Fries, Fungologist, 268.
Fritters of fungi, 314, 318.
Fungi. See, also, Toadstools, Mushrooms, and Moulds.
— by mail, 4, 5.
— Chemical constituents of, 14, 302.
— Classification of, 77, 78.
— Common tests for "Edible," and their reputation, 17–21, 24–29.
— Coral. See Clavaria.
— Crystals on, 227.
— Cultivation of, 85, 88. Bibliography, No. 8, 325 ; No. 23, 327.
— Desiccation of, 119, 246, 262, 301, 310, 321.
— Economic, 7, 13.
— Edible. See Agaricus Boletus, Clavarei, Fistulina, Helvella, Morel, Mushroom, and Puff-balls.
— Fastidiousness in vegetation, 86–88, 294.
— Gill-bearing (Agarics), 78, 178.
— Hawk fed upon, 302.
— Hygrometric properties of, 119.
— Insects infesting, 25, 29, 34, 36–38, 135.
— List of works on, 325.
— Medical, 277.
— Menu for fungus repast, 323.
— Miscellaneous, 231–274.
— Mycelium, or spawn, of, 44, 45, 77, 85, 88, 92, 107.
— Number of species of, 6, 30, 60.
— on caterpillars and chrysalids, 295.
— on chestnut-burr, 294.

Fungi on house-fly, 295.
— opposed to cultivation, 86–88.
— Ornamental forms of, 227.
— Phosphorescent, 227.
— Physiological features of, 15.
— Poisoning by, 2, 15, 29; diagnosis and treatment, 37; remedies, 38, 39; intoxication from, 59; antidotes, 62, 67, 68; report of poisoning case, 63–66; poisoning by contact and odor, 69; edible species inoculated by contact, 70.
— Popular distrust of, 15, 21.
— Rapid decay of, 6, 25, 30.
— Raw, eaten as salad, 248, 319.
— Recipes for cooking, 306–319.
— simulating animal food, 15, 30, 302.
— Spores and Spore-print of, 277–296.
— Study of, 7.
— traditions and superstitions, 22, 23.
— Vegetation of, 44, 47, 85–92, 107, 294.
— Whims of habitat of, 294.
Fungologists, Amateur, safe rules for, 33.
Fungus food in Europe and America, 8, 13–15, 35, 299.
— gnats, flies, and beetles, 37.

GASTEROMYCETES, 78.
Gathering mushrooms, Rules for, 35, 36.
Gautier, Dr. M. L., 62. Bibliography, No. 29, 327.
Germany, Fungus-eaters in, 14.
Gill-bearing mushrooms, 75–178.
Gnats infesting fungi, 37.
Greville, R. R. Bibliography, No. 19, 327.
"Grubs" in fungi, 25, 29, 34, 36–38, 135.

HARKNESS, Dr. H. W., 32, 245, 310. Bibliography, No. 5, 325.
Hawk fed upon Boleti, 302.
Hawthorne, Nathaniel, allusion to fungus phosphorescence, 228.

INDEX

Hay, William D. Bibliography, Nos. 20, 21, 327.
Heat destroys poison, 29, 72.
Hedgehog mushroom. See Hydnum.
Helvella crispa, 11, 231, 261, 262; other species, 11; recipes for cooking, 262, 316; to dry, 322.
Historical fungi, 43, 59, 60.
Hogg, Robert, LL.D. Bibliography, No. 15, 326.
Horse mushroom. See *Agaricus arvensis*.
House-fly fungus, 295.
Hungarian soup of Boleti, 314.
Hussey, Mrs. T. J., 40, 306, 310, 311, 315, 318. Bibliography, No. 10, 326.
Hydnei, 231–247; to cook, 310.
Hydnum, 300, 307;—*caput-medusæ*, 11, 27, 238–243; *repandum*, 11, 28, 232–238;—*rufescens*, 237, 238;—*coralloides*, 245;—*gelatinosum*, 319.
— Various edible species of, 11; to cook, 246.
Hygrometric fungus, 119.
Hygrophorus eburneus and *pratensis*, 11.
Hymenium of fungi, 78.
Hymenomycetes, 78.
Hyphomycetes, 78.

IDENTIFICATION of fungi, 31.
Idiosyncrasy, 30, 61.
Indigestibility of certain species, 30.
Inky mushroom, 28. See Coprinus.
Insects attacked by fungi, 295.
— infesting fungi, 25, 29, 34, 36, 38, 135.
Intoxication by Amanita, 59.
Introduction, 1.
Italy, Fungus-eaters of, 14, 86.

JELLY-LIKE mushroom, 319.
Johnson, Geo. W. Bibliography, No. 15, 326.

KAMCHATKA, Amanita dipsomaniacs of, 59, 60.
Ketchup, Mushroom. See Catsup.
Koppe, Dr., on Amanita poison, 60.

LACTARIUS, Poisonous, 61.
Lactarius, Various edible species of, 11; —*deliciosus*, 28, 166–171, 300, 311; —*piperatus*, 28, 171;—*volemum*, 171.
Lambs' kidneys, Flavor of, in fungi, 300, 311.
Letters to the author, 4.
Liver mushroom. See Fistulina.
Lucand, L. Bibliography, No. 30, 327.
Luminous fungi, 227.
Lycoperdaceæ, 267.
Lycoperdon. See Puff-ball.
— *bovista*, 11.
— structure of, 270.

MAILING fungus specimens, 4.
Marasmius,—*scorodoneus*, 11;—*oreades*, 11, 101–108;—*urens*, 108–111;—*peronatus*, 109–113.
McIlvaine, Captain Charles, 32; rule regarding edibility of fungi, 35; diagnosis and treatment of mushroom poisoning, 39, 40, 62; fastidiousness of fungi, 86, 184, 208. Bibliography, No. 6, 325.
Meadow Mushroom. See *Agaricus campestris*.
Medical and Surgical Reporter quoted, 62.
Medusa Mushroom. See Hydnum.
Menu of mushrooms, 323.
Microbes, 7.
Microscopic fungi, 7.
Mildew, 7, 78.
Milky mushroom. See Lactarius.
Miscellaneous fungi, 231–274.
Mock oyster soup, 306.
Moore, Justin P. Bibliography, No. 5, 325.
Moniteur Scientifique, quotation from, 61.

INDEX

Morchella esculenta. See Morel.
— *caroliniana*, 12.
Morel, 12, 231, 256; to cook, 316; to dry, 322.
Mortality in mushroom poisoning, 43.
Moss-mushroom, 245.
" Mother," 7.
Moulds, 7, 78.
Moyen, J. Bibliography, No. 31, 327.
" Muscarine " poison, 60.
" Mushroom " and " Toadstool," 16–21.
Mushrooms. See Toadstools, Agaricus, Boletus, Polyporei, Fistulina, and Fungi.
— à la crème, 308.
— à la Provençal, 308.
— Analysis of, 289–291.
— Baked, 311–313.
— Basket for, 36.
— Bibliography, No. 8, 325; No. 23, 327.
— Broiled, 308.
— by mail, 4.
— catsup, 320.
— Chemical nature of, 14, 61.
— Chestnut-burr, 294.
— Classification of, 77, 78.
— Cosmopolitan types of, 12.
— Cultivation of, 85, 86. Bibliography, No. 23, 327.
— Drying of, for food, 119, 246, 262, 301, 310, 321.
— Edible, 8, 13–15, 32.
— Edible species: plentiful supply of, 13, 35, 303; Beefsteak, 11, 27; Coral, see Clavaria; Elm, 10; " Fairy-ring," 95, 101; False Fairy-ring, 108, 109; Horse, 85, 91–95; Inky, 11, 20, 28, 88; Meadow, see *Agaricus campestris;* Milky, see Lactarius; Moss, 245; Oyster, see *Agaricus ostreatus;* Pasture, 10, 13, 113; Russulæ, 119–141; Spine-bearing, see Hydnum; St. George's, 95–101.

Mushrooms, Fastidiousness of most species of, 86, 294.
— Fried, 313, 317.
— Fritters of, 314, 317.
— Insects infesting, 25, 29, 34, 36–38, 135.
— Large specimens of, 92.
— List of works on, 325.
— Menu, 323.
— Melting. See Coprinus.
— Milky. See Lactarius.
— Moss. See Hydnum.
— Mycelium or spawn of, and vegetation of, 44, 45, 77, 85–88, 92, 107.
— Number of edible species of, 2, 7, 9, 32, 60; identification of, 2, 31; Curtis's list of, 9–12; nourishing properties of, 14; chemical simulation of animal food by, 15, 30, 302; popular tests for detecting, 22, 23; refutation of same, 24–29; desiccation of, 119, 321; recipes for cooking, 306–322.
— Number of general species of, 6.
— Pickled, 319.
— pie, 312.
— Poisonous species of, 2, 15, 17, 43–74; deadly species of, 2, 15, 43–74; poison by contact with, 30, 69; vinegar, sweet oil, and whiskey, 39; diagnosis and treatment of poisoning, 39, 63–66; historical poisoning by, 43, 59, 60; fatalities from, 43, 61; intoxication from, 59, 60; poison discriminated, 61; antidotes, 62, 67, 68; report of a poisoning case, 63–66; harmless mushrooms inoculated from poisonous, 70; salt, vinegar, and heat, 29, 39, 71, 72. See, also, Amanita, *Russula emetica*, Boletus, and False Champignon.
— Rapid decay of, 6, 25, 30.
— Roast, 311.
— Rules for gathering, 36, 70.
— Rural authorities on, 16–22.
— salad, 319.

INDEX

Mushroom soup, 306, 307, 323.
— spawn. See Mycelium.
— spores. See Spores and Spore-prints.
— Stewed, 307, 308–311, 315–317.
— tube. See Polyporei.
— Testing new species of, for edibility, 33.
— Whims of habitat of, 294.
Mycetes fungi, 77.
Mycology and mycophagy, 3, 4, 7, 8.
— Medical and economic, 7, 8, 13–15, 35, 277.
Mycophagists of America, 8, 9.
— Amateur, safe rules for, 38.

NERO, 59; poisonous mushrooms used by, 43.
Night, Fungi luminous by, 227
Nourishing properties of mushrooms, 14.

OAK-TONGUE fungus. See Fistulina.
Odor of Amanita poisonous, 69.
Omelet, Mushroom, 277, 278, 318.
Orcella, Agaric, 300.
Oyster mushroom, 10, 26, 27, 141–148; to cook, 303, 311, 315.
— flavor in fungi, 237, 247, 300, 303, 307, 310, 312.

Pachyma cocos, 11.
Palmer, Julius A., quoted: "Silver test," 25, 32, 40; on Amanita poison, 61, 69–71, 184, 207; on mushroom food, 303, 306, 311. Bibliography, Nos. 2, 3, 325.
Pasture, or parasol, mushroom, 9, 13, 80, 113.
Paulet, 306, 314.
Paxillus involutus, 11.
Payer, J. Bibliography, No. 27, 327.
Peck, Prof. Charles H., 32, 40, 182, 237, 246. Bibliography, No. 4, 325.
Persoon, 306, 316.
Phosphorescence in fungi, 227.

Pickled mushrooms, 319.
Pie of mushrooms, 312, 315.
Plates of the book, 39.
Pliny on mushroom "tests," 25 ; on poisonous mushrooms, 43, 59 ; on edible mushrooms, 298.
Poison-cup. See Amanita.
Poison of Amanita, 43, 61 ; antidote, 68 ; poisoning by contact and odor, 69.
Poisoning by fungi : Diagnosis and treatment, 38, 63, 68; vinegar as an antidote, 38, 71; antidote, 62, 68 ; Amanita, 2, 15, 43–74 ; poisonous species identified, 2, 15, 61 ; popular poison "tests" refuted, 17, 21–29 ; poisoning by contact, 30, 69.
Poisons, fatal and minor, 2, 15, 17, 29, 30, 61.
Polyporei, 78, 181–228; to dry, 321.
Polyporus, various edible species of, 11;
— *sulphureus*, 11, 219, 303; to cook, 316; botanical character of, 181–184, 285.
Popular discrimination between "toadstool" and "mushroom," 16–22 ; popular distrust of fungi, 15.
Pore-bearing mushrooms. See Boletus, Polyporei, and Fistulina.
Procerus mushroom, 10 ; pie of, 312.
Puff-ball fungi, 11, 13, 27, 78, 231, 267, 299; *gemmatum*, 268; *saccatum*, 268; *giganteum*, 268, 318; dissemination of spores of, 268, 277–280 ; medical use of, 277 ; as food, 277, 318 ; to cook, 318.
"Punk," 37, 181.
Purée of mushrooms, 307.

RAGOÛT of mushrooms, 309, 316.
Ravenel, H. W. Bibliography, No. 7, 325.
Recipes for cooking fungi, 72, 306–322.
"Ring" in mushrooms, 48, 85, 95.

Robinson, W., 306, 312, 313. Bibliography, No. 23, 327.
Roques, Joseph, 237, 306, 310, 311. Bibliography, No. 24, 327.
Rove-beetles infesting fungi, 37.
Rules for the venturesome, 33.
Russia, Fungus-eaters in, 14; fly Amanita in, 29.
Russula, 12, 13, 18, 26, 28;—*lepida*, 12, 127;—*alutacea*, 12, 133;—*virescens*, 12, 88, 120, 300;—*emetica*, 25, 27, 28, 61, 120, 122, 136–141;—*heterophylla*, 134, 300;—*ruber*, 300.
Russulæ, 119; opposed to cultivation of, 88; insects infesting, 135; to bake, 311; as salad, 319; to dry, 321.
Rust, 7.
Rustic fungology, 18–22.

SALAD of mushrooms, 319.
Salt as an antidote, 39, 72.
"Salt test" of mushrooms, 23, 29.
Scaly mushrooms. See *Amanita*, *Agaricus procerus*, and *Boletus strobiloides*.
Schmiedeberg, Dr., on Amanita poison, 60.
"Scotch Bonnet." See *Agaricus procerus*.
"Sep." See *Boletus edulis*.
"Seven Sisters of Sleep," by Rev. Dr. M. C. Cooke, 59.
Shadle, Dr. J. E., 62.
Shaggy-mane mushrooms, 11, 13; rustic appreciation of, 19, 27, 28. See *Coprinus comatus*.
"Shroud" in Amanita. 48.
Silver, Discoloration of, as a "test," 23.
Smith, Worthington T., 40, 306, 307, 309, 314. Bibliography, No. 14, 326.
Smuts, 7.
Socket in Amanita. See Volva.
Soufflé of puff-balls, 318.
Sparassis,—*crispa*, 12;—*luminosa*, 12.
"Spawn," or mycelium, of fungi, 44, 45, 77, 80, 85–88, 92, 107.

Specimens by mail, 5.
Spiders attacked by fungi, 295.
Spine-bearing mushrooms, 11, 27. See Hydnum.
Spore-prints from mushrooms, 44, 277–296; from *Amanita muscarius*, 287, 289; from Boletus, 285, 287; from *Agaricus campestris*, 283.
Spore surface, or hymenium, 78, 182.
Spores of fungi, 79, 87, 182, 268, 277–296; number of, 279; buoyancy of, 278–293; various colors of, 287; various forms of, 293.
Sporidiifera, 77, 231, 256.
Sporifera, 77, 78, 231, 256.
Staphylinus beetles infesting mushrooms, 37.
Stevenson, John. Bibliography, No. 22, 327.
Stew of fungi, 307, 308–311, 315–317.
St. George's mushroom, 95–101.
Strobilomyces, 202.
Styptic, Puff-balls used as, 277.
Sulphur mushroom, 219, 303; to cook, 316; as a salad, 319.
"Sweetbreads" in fungi, 300, 303.
Sweet-oil treatment for mushroom poisoning, 39.

TAYLOR, Thomas M. Bibliography, No. 8, 325.
Teeth-bearing mushrooms. See Hydnum.
Tertullian on toadstools, 17.
Testing new species for edibility, 33.
"Tests" or "proofs" for the detection of poisonous species, 17, 21–29.
Therapeutic Gazette, quotation from, 39.
Thore, Dr., quoted, 86.
Thread-like fungi, 78.
"Tinder,".37, 181.
"Toadstool" and "Mushroom," 16–21, 36; popular discrimination of, 16–24; popular tests for their discrimination and their refutation, 17–22, 24–

INDEX 337

29. See Mushroom, Fungi, Agaricus, Amanita, Boletus, Polyporei, Morel, Clavaria, Helvella.
" Toadstools," 181.
" Touchwood," 37, 181.
Tremella mesenterica, 12.
Tremelodon gelatinosum, 319.
Trichogastres, 231. See Puff-balls.
Tube mushrooms. See Polyporei, Boletus, and Fistulina.

VEGETARIAN, Menu for the, 304, 323.
Veil in mushrooms, 48, 60, 85.
Vigier, Dr., on Amanita poison, 60.

Vinegar as an antidote for mushroom poisoning, 39, 71.
Vitadini, 318.
Volva in Amanita, Importance of, in classification, 29, 33, 48, 77.

WARTY mushrooms. See Amanita, Pasture Mushroom, and *Strobylomyces*.
Wasps and bees, 36.
— Fungus attacking, 295.
Whiskey in mushroom poisoning, 39.
Wormy specimens of fungi, 25, 30, 34, 36–38, 135.

CPSIA information can be obtained
at www.ICGtesting.com
Printed in the USA
JSHW032038040322
JK11483500001B/28